A Review of
Mathematics Tests

A Review of Mathematics Tests

Jim Ridgway

NFER-NELSON

Published by The NFER-NELSON Publishing Company Ltd.,
Darville House, 2 Oxford Road East,
Windsor, Berkshire SL4 1DF

First published 1987
© 1987, Jim Ridgway

Typeset by First Page Ltd., Watford.
Printed by Billing & Sons Ltd., Worcester.

ISBN 0 7005 0679 9
Code 8186 02 1

Contents

Preface and Acknowledgements

Mathematical education is currently in the throes of a great deal of self-examination. In particular the *nature* of the mathematics which should be taught, the way it should be *taught*, and the way it should be *assessed*, are all subjects of much debate. I hope that this book, and its companion *Assessing Mathematical Attainment*, will make a useful contribution to this debate.

I embarked on this project after I had prepared reviews for *Tests in Education* edited by Philip Levy and Harvey Goldstein, but before publication of their book. That excellent volume covers a wide range of topics (for example tests of language, general abilities, personality and counselling) and is aimed at a more specialist audience. I would like to acknowledge my debt to both Professors for their practical support, and in particular to Phil Levy for stimulating my interest in the whole area of assessment when we worked together to produce tests for the selection of aircrew.

My interest in mathematical education developed when I worked at the Shell Centre for Mathematical Education as a visiting research fellow between 1981 and 1983, when the Testing Strategic Skills programme was established. Collaborative ventures have continued since then. I am pleased to acknowledge the contribution of everyone at the Shell Centre who has furthered my understanding of the relationship between assessment and education, and, in particular, to its Director, Hugh Burkhardt.

I am grateful to Anne Ridgway, John Gillespie, Barbara Binns and Alan Bell for comments on an earlier draft of this book. Shealagh Whytock, Sylvia Sumner, Sheila Whalley and Hazel

Satterthwaite put in valiant efforts typing and preparing the manuscript.

The book, written for teachers, is intended for the well-being of children – in particular, Emma, Alice and Rosemary.

Introduction

'You don't make a pig fatter by weighing it repeatedly.'
Lancaster headteacher

'Testing, whether written, oral or practical, should never be an end in itself, but should be a means of providing information which can form the basis of future action.'
Mathematics Counts, 1982

This book, together with its companion *Assessing Mathematical Attainment* sets out to offer guidance to anyone who is considering ways of testing mathematical skills. The main goals of this volume are to:

- raise issues about the purposes of testing;
- provide information about a variety of types of test, and the match between these and their intended purposes;
- offer guidance on choosing tests;
- offer reviews of individual tests.

Underlying these attempts to offer practical help are a range of purposes, common to both volumes, which have less tangible aims but which are at least as important. Some of these are to:

- encourage everyone concerned with mathematical education to consider the rôle of the assessment process;
- improve the quality of tests which are presently available;
- encourage more people to set out their own educational criteria, and to assess performance with respect to these criteria.

Tests here are conceived somewhat narrowly; to be included in this review, they must be commercially available from reputable publishers. As well as standardized mathematics tests, the volume contains reviews of mathematical progress, criterion referenced tests, tests of arithmetic skill, and diagnostic tests. It does not include reviews of examinations, tests used for research purposes, or practical tests; these are discussed (but not reviewed) in *Assessing Mathematical Attainment*.

The book is primarily intended for teachers of primary and secondary mathematics. No prior knowledge of the technicalities of test construction is assumed. A second group of users are those people not quite so directly involved with the education of children, such as headteachers, local education authority advisers and other staff engaged in administering the educational process. A third group of potential users comprises those professionals who service the education fraternity, such as educational psychologists, paediatricians – indeed, anyone who uses tests to understand more fully the individuals who present themselves. The fourth group for whom the book may prove to be of value are teachers undergoing training, who commonly receive instruction in the rationale underlying, and uses of, tests in education.

The first chapter, *Using this Volume*, contains advice on choosing a test or a series of tests; and a description of the contents of a test review. In order to choose tests rationally, some knowledge of the principles of test design, construction, trialling, and evaluation are necessary. These are dealt with in detail in the companion volume, *Assessing Mathematical Attainment*, and are described briefly in the test review. The review serves to illustrate the review format which is applied to each of the tests described in this book. It is hoped that the use of a common review structure will facilitate casual reference. It also points to features of tests and test manuals which affect their usefulness, and ease of use.

An effort has been made to avoid unnecessary use of the technical language which surrounds tests. Nevertheless, there is an important core of technical vocabulary which cannot easily be dispensed with because it captures neatly some important concepts. The *Glossary* provides a guide to all the technical terms used in the reviews.

A *Summary Table* at the back of the book allows an easy comparison of the broad features of all the tests reviewed.

Using this Volume

This book has been laid out so as to enable the user to locate tests suitable for their purposes in an efficient manner, and you are strongly advised to read this Chapter before you proceed further. There are three main stages in choosing a test:

- *specification* of the intended uses, and definition of the purposes for which test results will be used;
- *identification* of tests which might suit these purposes;
- *final selection*.

This volume has been arranged to provide guidance and help at each of these stages. Detailed test reviews are provided; these are arranged in alphabetical order and follow a common format to facilitate comparisons between tests. The reviews are supported by a *Summary Table*, designed to facilitate quick reference and to direct the user to those tests likely to be of central interest.

Why do you want to use a psychometric test?

In the present climate of scepticism about testing, it is as well to remember the obvious features of a test: namely, that items are publicly observable, and the scoring system is objective, and standardized. In this respect, it can be contrasted with many other ways of judging pupil performance, such as teacher impressions, which are likely to be based on a whole range of factors, not all of which concern the mathematical skills a pupil has actually mastered. Of course, test results should be used to supplement what is known about a child, not to replace this knowledge.

The three commonest kinds of tests are: norm referenced, criterion referenced, and diagnostic tests. A norm referenced test reports where a pupil stands with respect to other pupils who have taken the test. A criterion referenced test sets out to judge whether or not a pupil has been able to perform some well-defined task to an acceptable standard. A diagnostic test sets out to classify pupil conceptions and misconceptions. Different conclusions can be drawn from these different forms of test. For example:

norm referenced
Jo scored more marks on *Routes and Plans* than 85 per cent of a large national sample of 15-year-olds. Les has a standard score of between 70 and 80 on the *Routes and Plans* test.

criterion referenced
Jo can read timetables prepared by British Rail to a high degree of accuracy. She can make reasonable time estimates for a number of activities concerned with shopping and sightseeing (include examples). Les can locate large towns on Ordnance Survey maps. Les can use simple timetables (but not involving use of the 24–hour clock).

diagnostic
Jo has attained 'Level 5' understanding on the *Routes and Plans* test. She has no obvious conceptual misunderstandings. Les appears to interpret times on the 24-hour clock as base-ten decimals. He fails to allow time for changing trains, or for walking between shops.

These three uses are conceptually distinct. Test designers also embark on different methods of test development when they set out to produce tests of each type. For example, the development of diagnostic tests is likely to involve a great many interviews with pupils, in the search for common misconceptions; the development of norm referenced tests should involve large-scale testing of pupils representative of the school population as a whole. Nevertheless, *any* test can be used to produce *any* kind of interpretation. The key issue is the *purpose* of testing, and the way the test is used.

For example, if we assemble items related solely to whole number addition, and give this test to a class, we are likely to:

- calculate total scores and rank order pupils (norm referencing on a very small scale);
- praise pupils who score 95 per cent or more (criterion referencing, if we have spelt out our test design adequately);
- examine the scripts of poor performers, and talk to them, to see what they are doing wrong (diagnosis).

Norm referencing, criterion referencing, and diagnosis, have different purposes. These can be itemized as follows:

Norm referencing

1. Comparison with the standardizing sample, for such purposes as evaluating school performance with respect to a 'national standard'.
2. Making comparisons between schools, or between different educational treatments.
3. Comparing the effectiveness of different teachers by examining relative pupil gains after each year's teaching (or within school years, on parallel classes).
4. Rank ordering pupils for the purposes of: identifying children who are under-performing markedly (so that remedial action can be taken); identifying pupils of high attainment, for whom more elaborate challenges might be provided; grouping children (either into streams, or into mixed-ability classes).
5. Following pupil progress over time.
6. Taking account of differences in age when pupils are compared, since each pupil's standard score is based on a comparison with peers in the same narrow age band (say one month) rather than with the whole year group.

Of course, Purposes 1, 2, and 3 involve considerations other than test scores. For example, an evaluation of school performance would require some clear understanding about educational intentions; considerations of syllabus and curricular matters; knowledge about the catchment area; and so on. Such conceptual issues take more to resolve them than the administration of single, simple, measures!

Criterion referencing

1. Purposes 1,2,3,4,5 listed under norm referencing can often be satisfied by criterion referenced tests.
2. Specifying the nature of what has, and has not, been attained.
3. Identifying particular strengths and weaknesses of individual pupils, which can form the basis for personal work plans.
4. Identifying class strengths and weaknesses, to highlight topics that need more, and perhaps different, teaching effort.
5. Forming the basis for discussions with pupils, parents and colleagues.
6. Forming the basis for the transfer of information about pupils between schools.

Diagnostic testing

1. All the purposes listed under criterion referencing can often be satisfied by diagnostic tests.
2. Identifying specific pupil misconceptions which underlie particular errors (and sometimes describing teaching strategies to overcome these errors).
3. Describing hierarchies of conceptual development (which have implications for teaching).

These brief descriptions might be taken to suggest that one should always choose to use a diagnostic test, since it might well serve most of the purposes fulfilled by norm and criterion referenced tests. If only the choice were so simple! The virtues of diagnostic tests are bought at the cost of breadth of coverage. A 40-minute diagnostic test is likely to cover a narrow domain, such as fractions or vectors. A normative test is likely to attempt a much wider sampling across domains. This can be illustrated by comparing the content of the *Chelsea Diagnostic Tests* with, say, the Senior form of the *Graded Arithmetic-Mathematics Test* in the *Summary Table*.

How are the tests described here?

Having identified the purposes underlying your decision to employ a psychometric test, we should now consider characteristics of tests

Test Review

Author(s)
Dates of Publication;
Standardization; Revision
Publisher
Intended age range in years and
months (age range used during test
standardization, in years and months)
Form of administration
Timed/untimed; Duration
(estimate of duration)
Form of scores
Form of test

Item Distribution

	Number	Measurement	Space	Algebra	Logic	Statistics
Comprehension	–	–	–	–	–	–
Technique	–	–	–	–	–	–
Recall	–	–	–	–	–	–

Presentation

Words	Numbers	Algebra	Figures	Graphs	Pictures	Oral
–	–	–	–	–	–	–

Response

Free Format	Forced Choice	Constructed Lines	Explanation
–	–	–	–

Context

Abstract	Concrete	Total
–	–	–

This test review is presented solely to illustrate the review framework.

that are relevant to your needs. All the test reviews in this volume
follow a common format, shown above. This format will be used to
discuss the test characteristics.

Descriptions of test items

One can only decide what an individual test item assesses by a
programme of rather elaborate research. Even if some answer is
obtained, it is not always clear whether an item assesses precisely
the same skills in each individual. For example, many problems
can be represented in different ways, so pupils who draw diagrams
or graphs, or use algebra, are faced with different challenges by

the 'same' problem. Similarly, different degrees of expertise change the nature of the challenge faced. A problem that requires the routine exercise of technique for an older pupil can present a younger child with a challenge in creative problem solving. So the construct validity of any test cannot be determined easily, neither can it be assumed to be the same, irrespective of pupils' learning experience. Some judgements can, however, be made about the surface validity of a test item, and therefore of a whole test. If such judgements are used, their impressionistic nature must be stressed. Here, an attempt has been made to make such judgements, and to categorise test contents in tabular form.

The intention is to give test users an impression of the different balances of test content chosen by different test authors, in a way that is difficult to do by simple verbal description. Items are classified in terms of their *domain* (number, measurement, space, algebra, logic or statistics) and the *process* required (recall, technique or comprehension). They are also categorized as being set in a concrete context, or posed as abstract problems. The classification scheme is described below. Throughout, an effort has been made to judge contents in terms of the demands they place on the pupils for whom the test items are intended.

Domain

NUMBER
Counting and ordering; operations on integers, fractions, decimals and percentages; choice of operation; estimation and approximation; series; number bases.

MEASUREMENT
Reading and interpreting scales and tabular information; using instruments; knowledge of units; knowledge of size of units with respect to one's own experience; telling the time; using a calendar.

SPACE
Naming and recognizing plane and solid figures, and knowing their properties; calculating perimeters, areas and volumes; using scales, co-ordinates and bearings; general knowledge and use of geometry.

ALGEBRA
Using symbols; substituting in formulae; the idea of a variable; manipulation and solution of equations; obtaining a formula from a description in words; drawing graphs from formulas.

LOGIC
Satisfying multiple constraints; language, attributes, and use of sets; games and puzzles; reasoning.

STATISTICS
The calculation of averages; drawing inferences from data.

Process

RECALL
Remembering specific facts, definitions, concepts and formulae. For example, recall is involved in questions on the value of different digits presented in numbers; and calculation of areas and volumes where little numerical technique is required.

TECHNIQUE
The use of skills such as measuring, reading tables, geometric constructions, factorization, use of the four arithmetic operations, calculations involving fractions, decimals and percentages, where the task to be performed is quite explicit, but requires some skill which pupils could be reasonably expected to have acquired.

COMPREHENSION
The conversion of material presented in one form into another; the separation of relevant from irrelevant information in an item, for the purpose of solving problems; seeing implications of information presented. Comprehension is involved in problems such as: choice of operation; word problems; reasoning problems; combining information; completing series; interpreting information; explanation.

Items which involve only a single domain are categorized at the highest level that they assess. Comprehension items usually involve recall of factual knowledge and the deployment of technique – nevertheless, they are categorized solely as comprehension items.

Presentation

This refers to the appearance of items. Categories such as *Words, Numbers, Algebra, Figures, Graphs, Pictures* and *Oral* are mainly self-explanatory. Pictures differ from figures in that they are decorative, and have no obvious role in the mathematical processes required. For example, 'A bar of chocolate costs 25 pence. What would four bars cost?' might well be illustrated with a picture. In contrast, the item 'This block of chocolate is made up of a number of pieces. If four children share the block equally, how many pieces will each child have?' requires a figure.

Response

These categories describe the responses made by pupils. *Free Format* responses require pupils to construct answers from a potentially large set; *Forced Choice* responses constrain them to one of a set of fixed alternatives. *Constructed Lines* are drawn on diagrams by pupils; *Explanations* are verbal accounts (and are very rare in standard tests).

Context

Abstract refers to material presented in symbolic form only, such as numbers or letters. Diagrams are excluded. *Concrete* refers to material presented in a context familiar to the child; in the case of testing mathematical skills, this refers to problems which involve money, time, everyday objects etc. All items which involve units of measurement are labelled concrete.

A single item can involve a number of domains, and a variety of processes. For example, if pupils are presented with a diagram of geometric objects drawn on scaled squared paper, and are asked to calculate their volumes, this would be categorized as space/comprehension and measurement/technique and perhaps also as number/technique. It follows that both the sum of the numbers offered under *Domain*, and the sum of numbers offered under *Process* will almost always be greater than the total number of items presented in the test. In contrast, each item is categorized as being either abstract or concrete; the sum of the numbers under these two headings should always be the same as the entry under *Total*.

Test content should always be a prime concern. A danger associated with over-use of standardized tests of achievement is that they have an unfortunate effect on the kind of education which children receive. If scores on standard attainment tests are viewed with reverence by Local Education Authorities, school governors, parents and the like, then there will be pressure on teachers for their pupils to score highly on such tests. This 'backwash' effect can lead to an undesirable situation in which the school curriculum is shaped by the syllabus implied in the test items. This need not be a problem if the tests are carefully designed with a view to their educational impact (which is rarely the case) and if care is taken about the choice of tests in terms of test content, and if careful use is made of test scores.

Test summary data

The *Author, Dates of Publication, Standardization and Revision, Publisher,* and *Intended age range* are self-evident terms. All ages are shown in the form year:month – year:month. The *Age range used during test standardization*, shown in brackets, refers to the ages of pupils who took part in the standardization exercise; this age range ought to be close to the *Intended age range*. If it is not, the authors are making strong assumptions about test scores of some of the children in the *Intended age range*. Users should treat such tests with caution.

Form of Administration describes the method of test administration. Tests are commonly designed either for group or individual administration. Group tests can be given to individuals; tests designed for individual administration can rarely be given to groups.

Timed/untimed; Duration (estimate of duration) gives information on the time spent by pupils on the test. The total time taken for test administration will be longer, because of the need to settle the class, hand out forms, read instructions, and answer questions. In the case of untimed tests, an estimate of pupil test time is offered, based on suggestions in the manual, and on my own experience using the test.

Form of scores describes the methods used to report pupil performance, for example 'standard scores in one-month age bands'. Different kinds of test were described earlier; details of the different ways that scores are reported are given in the companion volume, *Assessing Mathematical Attainment*.

Form of test refers to the physical presentation of the test; for example: 'consumable booklets'; or 'test booklets and consumable answer sheets'.

Headings in the written review

Purposes

General purposes for testing were described earlier. Tests are designed for use with particular groups in mind, and for specific purposes; authors should state their intentions clearly. In these reviews, authors' purposes are quoted from test manuals, where possible. It is important to match one's own reasons for testing with the purposes for which the test was constructed. (Of course, a test author may well have failed to attain the goals aimed for – judgements on this issue can be found under *Evaluation*.)

Content

Descriptions of scales are given here, together with a summary of content which is intended to flesh out the summary data presented in tabular form. Tests can often be rejected because they fail to satisfy users' requirements about coverage of domains or processes (or for faults such as datedness of content, and technical inadequacy). Tests which appear to be suitable should always be inspected before widespread use. No test can include all the subskills that every teacher wishes to assess; tests should, therefore, assess abilities that teachers deem to be important.

Test development

ITEM PREPARATION

It can be assumed that authors have reasons for their choices of items. Too often, these reasons remain hidden from the test user. Test manuals should describe the principles which underlie the structure of the test, and describe each test item in terms of these principles. Preliminary trials of items, where discussed in the test manual, appear here.

STANDARDIZATION

This refers to the process of establishing a base-line of performance on the test, against which testees can be judged. It is a difficult and time-consuming process, and is rarely done well. Information should be presented on the nature and size of the standardizing sample, and about the population which this sample is intended to represent. The method of selecting the sample should be described; so too should the sample size. The date of testing is important; norms established in, say, September (at the start of the school year) will be different to norms established at other times of the school year. Ideally, if scores are to be compared with standardization data, testing should take place at the same time of year. Test manuals should provide explicit information about standardization dates.

Given a set of raw data, there are a number of ways of preparing standard scores. Manuals should describe, or refer to, the methods used. This is especially important when data are extrapolated to provide norms outside the age ranges from which raw scores were collected. Information should be provided on scores from different subgroups, most notably girls and boys. Two kinds of information are necessary: first, information about the mean performance level of each subgroup, and the spread of scores; second, about the increase in performance with age for each group.

All these issues are particularly important for norm referenced tests; they are less important for criterion referenced tests, and diagnostic tests, where the focus is on the identification of aspects of mastery. Even here, information about frequencies of different types of misconception, or ages at which pupils are likely to attain particular concepts, should be based on representative samples, if it is to be used for the purpose of comparison.

RELIABILITY AND VALIDITY

Reliability and validity are usually treated as discrete concepts, despite their intimate association. Each will be discussed under its own heading in the reviews. *Reliability* refers to the consistency of measurement. Two aspects of *reliability* are often considered; first, the extent to which testing the same children on different occasions gives similar results (usually called *test-retest reliability*); and second, the extent to which different parts of the same test assess similar skills (usually called *consistency*). These measures can be quite different. A test designer might construct a test aiming to sample a range of mathematical skills in a broad variety of domains; internal consistency might be quite low (by design), yet test-retest reliability might be high.

Validity is a complex issue. Several kinds of test validity can be described. *Surface validity* is what a test appears to measure; users can judge this for themselves. *Construct validity* refers to the extent to which a test matches its designer's intentions (in the example above, low internal consistency might be a requirement for high construct validity!) *Concurrent validity* refers to the extent to which test scores produce similar evaluations to other measures of the same thing. For example, concurrent validity can be established by comparing test scores to scores from other tests, or to teacher ratings. Showing that a test simply measures the same thing as other (ill-defined) tests is not very convincing; nor is an illustration that it tells teachers what they knew anyway. *Predictive validity* is measured by a test's ability to predict some outcome, such as examination success. The issues surrounding reliability and validity are discussed in more detail in *Assessing Mathematical Attainment*.

Using the test

Describes the test *administration*, and includes information on recommended users, materials required, and the adequacy of the script provided. The section on *scoring* offers comments on scoring instructions, the scoring key provided, ease of use, and the form of recording scores. *Interpretation of results* discusses the way errors of measurement are treated; the relationship between recommended uses of scores and the original purposes of the test; any cautionary advice offered; and advice offered for action on the basis of results.

Evaluation

In contrast with earlier sections, which are intended to describe a test clearly in a detached way, the *Evaluation* section offers a judgement on the test, based on a consideration of all the earlier sections. In particular, it offers an evaluation of the test – in terms of its technical competence and of the extent to which it might satisfy the purposes for which it was designed.

Test descriptions in the summary table

Much of the data described above is presented in the *Summary Table*, which appears as *Appendix 4* (page 195); this table contains, additionally, estimates of the cost of testing. Tests and test series appear in order to the youngest pupils for whom they are designed, so that would-be users can locate all the tests that might be relevant to their purposes, relatively easily. The headings in the *Summary Table* are, for the most part, self-explanatory, although some require a brief description, and the codes used under different headings need to be described.

Name: name as it appears on the test, and in the review.

Age range: the age range shown is the range claimed by the manual; the age range of pupils who took part in the standardization exercise is given in the review. All ages are shown in the form years:months – years:months. Tests which quote ages of 16:00 and above are usually described as suitable for assessing adult performance. Restrictions on test use are indicated by the presence of *R* in the age range column.

Content: has already been described. The category system used in the *Test Review* is repeated here, although some data are condensed.

Administration: tests are often designed to be administered either to individuals (*I*) or to groups (*G*). While group tests can easily be administered to individuals, tests designed for individual administration can rarely be given to groups. Most tests are presented in written form, although some are given orally (*O*), especially those intended for younger pupils, or pupils with reading difficulties. Codes can be combined; so *IO* is a test administered orally to an individual pupil, and *G* is a group test presented in written form.

Time: For timed tests, the time taken to administer the test is given in minutes. For untimed tests, where an estimate of testing time is offered in the test manual, it is shown in parentheses (*45*); otherwise it is denoted (–).

Form of scores: Different methods of reporting scores are described in the *Glossary*. They have been coded: Criterion Referenced (*C*); Diagnostic (*D*); Score Frequency Distributions (*F*); Levels of Understanding (*L*); Mathematical Age (*M*); Percentiles (*P*); Profiles (*Pr*); Standard Scores (*S*); Stanines (*St*). Codes can be combined, e.g. *S,P,D*.

Latest revision: Provides the date of the most recent test revision.

Cost: Provides a rough guide to cost. The first column gives some idea of the cost of a specimen set (manual, scoring key, pupil booklet, etc.); the second column gives a rough indication of the cost of a single pupil booklet. Costs under both headings are allocated into one of the three bands: relatively cheap (*C*); moderate (*M*); and relatively expensive (*E*). Codes are derived from publishers' prices obtained in 1986, and so are subject to change.

The values were then as follows

	Specimen	*Booklet*
C	£0 – £5	0 – 25p
M	£5 – £10	25p – 50p
E	£10+	50p+

Page: Gives the page number of the test review.

Choosing tests

Users requiring a test for one-off use will have different needs to those who want a series of tests spanning a number of classes (who may also wish to monitor progress through the school). Advice on these two uses will be offered separately.

Choosing a single test

The first test feature to consider is the pupil *age range* that the test is designed for. Tests and test series appear in the Table in age order, as given by the author. The first test in the Table is suitable for use with the youngest children; the last test has the highest-starting minimum age. These age ranges need not be the age ranges on which the tests were standardized; the ages of the pupils used during test standardization are given in parentheses in the test reviews themselves. A large discrepancy between the two might give cause for concern. Considering only tests suitable for particular ages will narrow the choice of tests considerably.

Cost should be considered next; it is not really worth considering using a test that the school cannot afford! Test *contents* should be considered, along with the *form of scores*. Having read the earlier discussion about different purposes of testing, and different forms for reporting scores, you should be able to make an informed choice of the reviews worth reading in detail in the light of your purposes, and the curriculum followed by your pupils (which can be compared with test contents). For example, users who require tests of basic number skill, which require little comprehension or knowledge of how these skills can be applied, can locate such tests by looking for tests with a predominance of items in the *Number* column and the *Knowledge* and *Technique* rows. Users who require an assessment of a range of mathematical skills at all levels from knowing simple facts to deploying these skills in applied contexts, should look for a spread of items across all the cells of the Table.

Next read the *Evaluation* sections of each candidate test; you may be able to reject some candidate tests on the basis of my evaluations. Alternatively, you might choose to read the whole test review to understand more fully the basis of the evaluation. Finally, an early Latest Revision date might give pause for thought about the likely datedness of the test content.

Before making a final decision about your choice of test(s), please read the complete test review.

Choosing a series of tests

Tests constructed to form part of a series usually have similar titles, and are grouped together in the *Summary Table*. Check that the pupil ages for which the test is designed are appropriate, and overlap. The issue of the purpose of testing should be discussed with everyone involved in teaching, and should be allied to discussions about curriculum matters, and the uses to which test scores will be put. Choosing a series of tests, of course, compounds all the problems of choosing a single test. Every series has some tests that are better designed than others; it may well be necessary to tolerate a test for, say, 10-year-olds, which has some known weaknesses, in order to obtain results that are comparable with satisfactory tests in the same series available for seven, eight, nine and 11-year-olds.

You are strongly advised to obtain specimens of the tests under consideration, so that informed judgement can be made about the suitability of the test items for your purposes.

APU ARITHMETIC TEST

S.J. Closs and M.J. Hutchings
First Published 1976; Standardized 1973
Hodder and Stoughton, UK
11:00–18:11 (11:00–18:11)
Group
Timed; 25 mins
Raw Scores; Percentile Ranks in one-year age bands
Consumable booklets

Item Distribution

	Number	Measurement	Space	Algebra	Logic	Statistics
Comprehension	20	–	6	–	7	9
Technique	25	2	–	–	–	–
Recall	3	–	–	–	–	–

Presentation						
Words	Numbers	Algebra	Figures	Graphs	Pictures	Oral
40	50	–	7	3	–	–

Response			
Free Format	Forced Choice	Constructed Lines	Explanation
57	3	–	–

Context		
Abstract	Concrete	Total
39	21	60

*Note that the test was produced at the Applied Psychology Unit at the University of Edinburgh, **not** at the Assessment of Performance Unit of the DES.*

Purposes

The *APU Arithmetic Test* is designed to fulfil the 'need for an instrument which can be used by non-mathematicians who are concerned with advising people about educational or vocational choices or with the selection and training of personnel for jobs in which numeracy is an important factor. In these instances what is required is ... an overall indication and achievement in arithmetic which ... is sufficiently reliable to provide a basis for accepting a course or a job as at least a possibility worth considering, or for ruling it out as distinctly improbable as a realistic choice.'

The Manual states clearly that the Test is not intended to sample a wide range of mathematical skills, such as those involved in geometry, calculus and the use of matrices. When this wider range of skills needs to be sampled (for example, when advising on career choices which might involve the use of mathematical skills in the social sciences, business or engineering) it recommends that such assessment should be left to professional teachers of mathematics.

'... essentially an *achievement* test and not an *aptitude* test.'

'It can be used with less able pupils and with fifth and sixth formers, but is likely to be less sensitive than tests which are specifically designed for such groups.'

Content

Despite the title, the contents cover a wide range of mathematics topics where arithmetic is involved; the test is *not* a measure of the ability to do 'hard sums'. The Test aims to suit a wide age range: consequently the item difficulties span a wide range, too. Topics include: basic arithmetic operations on whole numbers; decimals; fractions; powers; percentages; series; ratio; and probability. Many items are made easier by confident use of algebra, although several of these can be solved by trial and error methods.

Test development

'The item content has been chosen to give a fair coverage of the topics in arithmetic which are typical of the modern school mathematics syllabus ... note, however, that ... only arithmetic topics are sampled ...'

'... items have been designed so that a minimum of calculation is required and the spread of difficulty is such that the test is most sensitive to differences in achievement among average to just above average pupils.'

No information is provided about **item preparation**, nor about early trialling of the materials, nor about the authors intentions and principles in item construction. However, the authors encourage potential users to inspect test items, in order to decide if the set of items presented here is an adequate reflection of the mathematics curriculum of the persons to be tested.

The Test was **standardized** using a sample of 14 schools, chosen to represent small, medium and large schools equally. These schools were chosen from a wide range of geographical sites throughout the UK. Despite the authors' efforts, this is probably rather a small number of schools to justify their reference to 'a national sample'.

Test results from 6393 pupils ranging from 11 to 18 years of age were used. The spread across ages was somewhat uneven; relatively small samples were available from the 11–, 16–, 17– and 18–year-old ranges. The Manual urges caution in the interpretation of the percentiles for the older children identified. The 16+ group were still at secondary school at the time of testing: the group therefore consisted largely of pupils staying on to take leaving certificate examinations and intending to go on to further study (that is, a selected group of above-average ability). The Manual points to the difficulty of gathering scores from the 16+ age group who are not at school, and sensibly advises test users to use the school-leaving age of the person being tested as the basis for obtaining their percentile score. (The Manual also points to t' e crudeness of this procedure.)

Percentiles are shown for each raw score, within one-year age bands. No information is given about sex differences in performance, nor about the distribution of ages by sex within the standardization sample.

The problem of errors of measurement are discussed; the Manual shows how the SEM depends on both the reliability of the test, and the score variance. It points out that the SEM is likely to be different for different age groups taking the Test, and shows SEMs for each age group. It also describes clearly how these SEMs should be used in the recording and use of test scores. Unfortunately, the derivation of these SEMs is unsatisfactory.

Test-retest reliability was assessed on the basis of a sample of 182 13–year-old pupils tested on two occasions separated by one week. This is probably too short an interval, and the resulting correlation of 0.96 probably overestimates the reliability of the Test. Analysing the table, it appears that all the SEMs for different ages, reported in the Manual, are based on the reliability coefficient derived for 13–year-olds. **Internal consistency** was computed for a sample of 214 pupils in the age range 15 to 16; using a measure like KR–20, the coefficient was found to be 0.91.

Since this is an achievement test, the authors assert that the **test validity** is best assessed by looking at the item content: if this adequately samples the arithmetic curriculum, and so long as standardization is satisfactory, they argue that the test can be assumed to be valid. They urge the test user to look at test items and see if this is the sort of thing they want to measure.

The correlation with the *Graded Arithmetic-Mathematics Test* for a sample of 142 13–year-old pupils was 0.88. An interesting feature of the Manual is the report of correlations of the *APU Arithmetic Test* with both Scottish Certificate of Education (SCE) Leaving Certificate examination results, and General Certificate of Education (GCE) examination results: each of these was based on a large sample of pupils selected carefully at random. Some of these correlations were surprisingly high. For example, between SCE 'O' Grade: Arithmetic (0.75); Mathematics (0.65); Physics (0.63); Applied Mechanics (0.59). Correlations with SCE Higher Grade examinations were modest: (Mathematics (0.45); Chemistry (0.51); Physics (0.48)). Correlations with GCE 'O' level results were lower still. For example, Mathematics (0.39); Physics (0.34); Chemistry (0.31). The different magnitude of correlation between Scottish and English examinations with the *APU Arithmetic Test* might be explained if the item content more closely relates to Scottish examination syllabuses than it does to English ones.

Using the test

The authors provide some good cautionary notes on the misuse of tests, guidance on how to use this test and score it, and references to further reading. Sensible advice is offered about the need to time the test accurately; to prevent cheating; to establish a good relationship with those being tested; to avoid providing clues to answers to questions; on the need to explain why the subject is being tested; to be unobtrusive or neutral in the testing situation.

The procedure for **administration**, described in the Manual, is perfectly adequate for using the test. The instructions for the pupil are presented on the front of the booklet and are self-explanatory. Administration requires a stopwatch, test booklets, and pencils. Instructions for **scoring** are quite clear; the Manual is explicit about alternative answers which are and are not acceptable. Scoring keys are easy to use; scores are written on the front of the test booklet. The Manual explains how percentile ranks are obtained. Obtaining ranks for the scores of each pupil, given their age, is simple. **Interpretation** of scores is obvious.

Evaluation

The Test presents 60 items, which cover a wide range of mathematical topics, with the intention of scanning the 11– to 18–year-old population. Consequently, the test is a 'broad-brush' index of attainment, rather than a carefully-honed diagnostic instrument.

A strong point of the test content is that it samples the use of arithmetic operations in a wide variety of domains; this focus on the ability to know which operations to use under which circumstances should rightly be considered to be an important component of arithmetic skill. It is certainly well worth including this variety of domains, rather than focusing exclusively on the ability to manipulate increasingly unwieldy numbers.

The Manual is well written, lucid, and states quite clearly the designers' intended use for the Test. Its attention to the problems of administering tests, and to the interpretation of test results (including treatment of error of measurement) are commendable. A good deal of effort went into the standardizing sample. The caveats in the Manual about inappropriate use of tests, together with the designer's intention to educate all classes of test users about the nature of psychometric measurement, are certainly worthy of imitation by other authors. This test meets quite satisfactorily the aims of the test authors, as defined in the Manual.

BASIC MATHEMATICS TEST A

National Foundation for Educational Research
First Published 1971; Standardized 1975
NFER-NELSON, UK
6:09–8:06 (6:09–8:02)
Group, Oral
Untimed; (45 mins)
Standard Scores in one-month age bands; some diagnostic use
Consumable booklets

Item Distribution

	Number	Measurement	Space	Algebra	Logic	Statistics
Comprehension	13	7	5	–	1	–
Technique	9	5	3	–	–	–
Recall	–	–	1	–	–	–

Presentation						
Words	Numbers	Algebra	Figures	Graphs	Pictures	Oral
36	31	–	19	7	2	40

Response			
Free Format	Forced Choice	Constructed Lines	Explanation
26	12	2	–

Context		
Abstract	Concrete	Total
10	30	40

Purposes

'... aims to measure children's understanding of the fundamental relationships and processes which form the basis of all mathematical work.'

'... to provide a measure of how well a child has grasped and developed the ideas he has met in the early part of his junior school.'

'... to give some diagnostic information about a child's individual strengths and weaknesses ...'

'It is hoped ... that the test results can be interpreted as reasonably "pure" measures of mathematical attainment.'

Content

Forty items cover the use of a number of mathematical operations across a wide range of topic areas. The operations represented are equating; counting; adding; ordering; subtracting; and with just two questions to each, classifying, multiplying and dividing. These operations are applied to a variety of topics (quantities, ideas or domains), namely size; shape; volume; fractional parts; the interpretation of bar charts and pictograms; place value; area; money; length; weight; and time (reading a clock). Scores can be derived for each operation and for each topic. Items consist of clear line drawings.

Test development

No data are available on how the items were prepared, nor is there any information about piloting studies that may have been conducted. Clues about the construct validity of each item can be obtained by examining the diagnostic scoring scheme for each item.

The Test was **standardized** on 6,073 children (3,178 boys, 2,895 girls) from two areas: an urban area in the Midlands, and a London Borough, with a mean age of 8:06. The Manual claims that these data 'give a fair approximation to the "national standard"'. The sample size is adequate, but is unlikely to be representative of the whole school population.

The Manual provides a guide to the interpretation of standard scores in terms of the percentage of children who attained less than a given standard score.

Neither differences in terms of raw scores between boys and girls, nor in terms of the increase of score with age were found to be significant; a common set of norms, therefore, is provided.

The only reported **reliability** test is that of internal consistency (KR–20) which was found to be 0.91. The sample consisted of 261 individuals chosen randomly from one of the areas taking part in the standardization. A value of 0.91 corresponds to a standard error of measurement of 4.54, at the mean age of 7:06. Caution should be exercised, since no adjustment for age or ability differences over the two-year age range is offered. The Manual explains how this value is to be interpreted and used when comparing individuals, in a straightforward manner. No **validation** studies are reported. Inspection of the test items, however, taken together with the profile scoring scheme, provides strong clues about the content validity of the test items. Since the Test is a measure of mathematical attainment, rather than of some mystical latent trait of mathematical ability, parallel items are easy to construct.

Using the Test

The Test is **administered** orally to overcome the problems which poor readers face when presented with written mathematics problems. The Test requires pupils to understand spoken English, and to possess elementary writing skills. Children need a response booklet, a pencil and an eraser. 'The proper administration of an oral test requires particular skill, and it is recommended that this test should be given by an experienced teacher.' Questions are read aloud by the test administrator, one item at a time. The time taken to administer the Test depends on the speed of the slowest child in each group. The Manual recommends that the Test be administered in two parts, separated, perhaps, by the mid-morning break. The Test should not be given to a group of more than 40 children. The script (provided in the Manual) for administering the Test is perfectly clear for the administrator.

Instructions for **scoring** the Test are also clear. The test booklet contains a well set-out score summary sheet. The scorer's discretion for the acceptance of a 'wrong' answer is specified unambiguously. Reversal of numbers, mirrored numbers and misspelled words are permitted. The scoring procedure offers some checks against scorer errors.

An overall raw score is calculated for each script, which can be converted to a standard score. The score summary sheet provides a box labelled 'score band' – a useful reminder to the user of the errors inherent in measurement, and of the dangers of over-inter-preting small differences between pupils.

The scoring scheme also offers a profile of the mathematical attainment of each pupil. Each question in the Test is identified as assessing skills relevant to at least one operation and to at least one topic. A simple checklist, completed while scoring the Test, allows the child's scores on each operation, and each topic, to be determined.

Interpretation of test results is direct. Raw test scores and standard scores can provide a rough idea about overall class performance compared to classes in an urban area in the Midlands and in a London Borough. They can also be used to rank children within a class in order of their mathematical attainment. At least as useful is the prospect of identifying areas of relative weakness, both of individuals and of the whole class, to enable remedial action to be taken. The classification of test items into scores on different topics and on the use of different operations provides a strong indication of the nature of the difficulty experienced.

Evaluation

The Test provides a source of feedback for the class teacher – about teaching performance and about the needs of individual pupils. The Manual is clearly written, and provides a straightforward guide to test use. A good feature is the use of a score *band* for each individual, rather than a score.

The test booklet is clear and easy to use. The test items are, by and large, unambiguous – although a minor amendment could usefully be made: Questions 3 and 4 show a triangle which should be dissected exactly, but is not.

The diagnostic uses of the Test are sometimes limited by the small number of items devoted to several topics, which will result in low reliability of the individual assessments. The manual invites comments on the usefulness of this scheme, but offers no information about how it has been used so far. Hopefully, future editions of the Manual will contain such information.

Using the Test diagnostically may prove to have benefits beyond the immediate test scores obtained. An obvious benefit is to allow the teacher to pinpoint topics that have not been dealt with adequately in lessons (or that may not have been covered at all). A less obvious benefit may come simply from the teacher's analysis of the items into operations and topics, and the translation of the analysis into classroom mathematical activities. A notion which should be central to mathematical learning is the applicability of mathematical operations across a wide range of topics both inside and outside the classroom. If this Test causes us to increase the number of topics used to illustrate the different mathematical operations, and thus help pupils generalize the rules they learn, it will have served a very useful function.

Another good feature of the Test is the transparency of the rules for item construction. Teachers should be able to generate parallel items, easier items, and more difficult items, all with similar construct validity, for teaching and reassessment purposes. This process of de-mystifying tests is useful in itself. Since the Test is an *attainment* test, it should be clear just what is being attained. A focus on 'attainment', rather than 'ability' casts the teacher in the role of transmitter of knowledge, rather than observer of human intellectual development.

This test is similar in format to *Mathematics Attainment Test A*, which is also reviewed in this volume. *Basic Mathematics Test A* should be used in preference to that test because of:

- its potential use as a diagnostic test;
- the attention devoted to analysing items;
- the wider spread of operations across topics.

BASIC MATHEMATICS TEST B

National Foundation for Educational Research
First Published 1971; Standardized 1973; Manual Revised 1976
NFER-NELSON, UK
8:04–9:10 (8:07–9:07)
Group, Oral
Untimed; (45 mins); split into two parts
Standard Scores in one-month age bands; some diagnostic use
Consumable booklets

Item Distribution

	Number	Measurement	Space	Algebra	Logic	Statistics
Comprehension	16	10	10	–	7	–
Technique	5	3	1	–	–	–
Recall	–	–	–	–	–	–

Presentation						
Words	Numbers	Algebra	Figures	Graphs	Pictures	Oral
35	31	–	19	5	3	40

Response			
Free Format	Forced Choice	Constructed Lines	Explanation
21	15	4	–

Context		
Abstract	Concrete	Total
12	28	40

Purposes

'… the second in a series of tests which have been developed … to cover the age range 7–15 years.'

The Manual states that the test authors have attempted to 'eliminate, as far as possible, the effect of different teaching methods'. It is hard to imagine how this can be achieved, or indeed if it is possible. In other respects, the stated purposes are identical to those for *Basic Mathematics Test A*.

Content

Forty items cover the use of a variety of mathematical operations, representing equating; ordering; adding; subtracting; counting; dividing; multiplying and classifying. The operations are applied to the topics of: shape; relations; interpretation of a pictogram; volume; size; length; area; fractions; with just one question each addressed to permutation, approximation, place value, weight and time. Scores can be derived for each operation and for each topic.

Test development

No data are available on how the items were prepared, nor is there any information about piloting studies which may have been conducted. Clues about the construct validity of each item can be obtained by examining the diagnostic scoring scheme for each item.

The Test was **standardized** on 6,878 children (3,563 boys, and 3,315 girls) in two urban areas, one in West Yorkshire, and one in the Midlands, with a mean age of 9:01. The conversion table in the Manual shows the standardized score of an individual child, given the child's age and raw test score. The Manual provides a guide to the interpretation of these standard scores in terms of the percentage of children who attained less than a given standardized score. The authors state that the data were considered insufficient for establishing a national standard with confidence. They advise the user to remember the nature of the sample when interpreting and using the norms provided. Neither differences of raw scores between boys and girls, nor differences in the increase of score with age were found to be significant. A single set of norms is provided.

The only reported **reliability** coefficient is that of internal consistency (KR–20), which was found to be 0.91. The sample consisted of 362 individuals chosen randomly from one of the areas taking part in the standardization study. A value of 0.91 corresponds to a standard error of measurement of 4.51 at mean age 9:01. The Manual explains how this value is to be interpreted and used when comparing individuals, in a straightforward manner. No **validity** studies are reported. Inspection of the test items, together with the profile scoring scheme, provides strong clues about the content validity of the Test.

Using the Test

Administration of the Test is oral, to overcome the problems that poor readers face when presented with written mathematics problems. Details about the administration are identical to those provided for *Basic Mathematics Test A*. Unlike *Test A*, this Test suggests that the children should simply fill in their names on the front cover, and that the teacher should complete the rest of the details later. Clearly this advice is sensible; it should be incorporated into the Manual for *Test A*.

Test administration requires test booklets, pencils, and erasers. The Manual provides advice on testing, and a script for administering the Test – both of which are perfectly clear.

The **scoring scheme** follows that described for *Basic Mathematics Test A*, and is to be commended for its clarity, ease of administration, and use of a score band, rather than a single score for each individual.

Test results make **interpretation** easy. Scores can be compared to scores obtained elsewhere (although not to a 'national sample'). They can be used to compare children within each class, taking account of age differences, and they can play a diagnostic rôle in unravelling children's misunderstandings, and in identifying curriculum topics which need more attention.

Evaluation

See *Basic Mathematics Test A* for a more general evaluation. This test is similar in content to *Mathematics Attainment Test B* and since it was developed from that Test, should be used in preference to it.

Test items are, by and large, unambiguous, although two minor amendments could usefully be made:

a) *Question 4*
   In question 4, both the Manual and the Test itself refer to Picture A and Picture B, although none of the pictures are labelled B. (However, most children will have no difficulty in identifying Picture B.)

b) *Question 21*

Question 21 is a weighing problem. A scale pan is shown with a 100 gram weight in it, which is clearly heavier than the block of wood which is to be weighed. The question asks the children to find the exact weight of the wood by choosing one from a set of four alternative weights. These weights are 50 grams, 90 grams, 110 grams, and 150 grams. According to the Manual, the correct answer is 90 grams. In my discussions with children who wrote down 50 grams as the correct answer, they asserted that when weighing, it is important to get the unknown weight into a bracket, rather than simply guessing what its correct weight might be. This item should be revised.

The diagnostic aspects of the Test are rather limited because of the small number of data points for many of the topics. (For example, permutation, approximation, place value, weight, and time, are assessed with a single question each.) The Manual provides no information about the usefulness of this diagnostic information, but invites comments on the effectiveness of this scheme; hopefully, later editions of the Manual will include discussion about the usefulness of these diagnostic aids based on teachers' studies.

The review of *Basic Mathematics Test A* eulogized over the potential of diagnostic tests for the identification of individual problems on topics, the wide range of topics which each mathematical operation was applied to, and the transparency of the rules for item construction. The same eulogy may be applied to this test.

This is one of the most satisfactory tests to be found for assessing the mathematical attainment of this age group.

BASIC MATHEMATICS TEST C

National Foundation for Educational Research
First Published 1970; Standardized 1971–2; Manual revised 1972
NFER-NELSON, UK
9:07–10:10 (9:08–10:09)
Group
Untimed; (50 mins)
Standard Scores in one-month age bands; some diagnostic use
Consumable booklets

Item Distribution

	Number	Measurement	Space	Algebra	Logic	Statistics
Comprehension	23	1	7	–	6	–
Technique	9	5	3	2	7	–
Recall	–	–	–	–	–	–

Presentation						
Words	Numbers	Algebra	Figures	Graphs	Pictures	Oral
48	43	3	17	6	–	–

Response			
Free Format	Forced Choice	Constructed Lines	Explanation
30	16	4	–

Context		
Abstract	Concrete	Total
22	28	50

Purposes

'... the third in a series of tests which have been developed to cover the age range 7–15 years.'

'... scores ... will give a fairer basis for comparison than those yielded by our Mathematics Attainment Tests.'

'... aims to measure children's understanding of the fundamental relationships of processes which form the basis of all mathematical work. The questions are designed to eliminate as far as possible the effects of different teaching methods ...'

Content

Fifty items cover a number of mathematical operations spread across a wide range of topic areas. The operations represented are multiplication; addition; division; subtraction; reflection; equality; equivalence; order; use of number patterns and number bases. Topics covered are vulgar fractions; fractional parts; decimals and percentages; shape; area; length and volume; Venn diagrams; histograms, line graphs and 3–D drawings; set membership and set intersection.

The test booklet is attractively presented. The language used is quite accessible to children of average ability within the age group for which the test is designed.

Test development

No information is given about the origins of the items, nor is any information presented about item selection or pre-pilot trials which may or may not have been carried out.

The Test was **standardized** on all third-year children in primary schools in two unspecified areas. 4,371 boys and 4,175 girls took part in the study, with a mean age of 10:02.

There was a small raw score difference in favour of girls, which was not statistically significant. When the small age differences between girls and boys was taken into account, the direction of the difference was reversed. However, the age allowances to be made for boys and girls were found to be significantly different – and therefore separate conversion tables are provided.

A random sample of 397 children (age composition unspecified) was used to calculate KR–20, a measure of *internal consistency*, which was found to be 0.95. At mean age 10:02 this gives a value of 3.30 for the standard error of the Test. The Manual explains how this value is to be interpreted, and in a straightforward fashion. The Manual also gives guidance about the standard error of the Test at different ages.

No evidence is presented about the **validity** of the Test. Inspection of the test items themselves, together with the profile scoring scheme, offers clues about the content validity of the Test.

Using the Test

Preparations for the Test are clearly laid out and sensible. Pupils need a test booklet, pencils and a ruler. Details of the administration are perfectly adequate. The Manual sensibly suggests that the teacher should fill in the child's age on the answer booklet. Instructions for scoring are unambiguous. The marking sheet is clearly laid out: however, the marking sheet would be easier to use if the spacing between questions were identical to that on the Test itself, as is the case in other tests of this series. The scoring sheet allows separate totals for right and wrong answers, together with a check sum on the total number of questions on each page, to help avoid marker errors.

Instructions on the use of the conversion of raw scores to standardized scores are clear. The table of norms allows the score of each individual testee to be compared to the scores obtained by a large sample of children of the same age.

The **interpretation** of standard scores in terms of the proportion of children who will exceed these standard scores is only briefly explained in the manual; tabular presentation, used to explain standard scores found in other manuals in this series, is to be preferred.

Providing standardization tables in which raw scores are converted to standardized scores correct to the nearest integer can leave the reader with a feeling that the Test is spuriously accurate. The practice of entering the child's standard score as a pair of numbers which bracket the score, used in other tests in this series, should be used here.

Evaluation

See *Basic Mathematics Test A* for a more general evaluation.

The Test was developed from tests in the *Mathematics Attainment* series, and should be used in preference to those tests.

The claim that the test has been designed to 'eliminate ... the effects of different teaching methods' seems too grand. Can we really assess the cognitive processes that underlie mathematics in a way which is divorced from any particular curriculum? More modest claims should be made about the designer's intentions.

Test users should be encouraged to examine test items in order to decide if these are the sort of tasks that they would like the childrens' classroom experiences to generalize to.

The Test covers a wide variety of mathematical topics in quite an interesting way. The material is well presented, and seems to appeal to children. The instructions for test administration and scoring are clear, and the Test is easy to use.

Three amendments could be made to the scoring key (1980 printing):

a) *Question 35*
From the answer given to Question 35 we learn that $18 - 7 = 3 + 3!$

b) *Question 47*
In Question 47 pupils are given a time-distance graph and are asked to read the time at which a certain distance was reached. Due to slight inaccuracies in printing, the most accurate estimates of the time taken do not fall in the centre of the bracket of acceptable answers given in the Manual.

c) *Page numbers*
The page numbers in the key do not correspond to the page numbers in the test itself.

The Manual is seriously deficient in a number of ways: no information is provided about the uses to which the Test may be put, nor about the diagnostic scoring scheme. Information on the nature of the standardizing sample is omitted; little guidance is given to users about the way that scores should be interpreted. A revised version of this Manual, developed along the lines of other tests in this series, should be issued. In the meantime, users would be well advised to use the Manual for *Basic Mathematics Attainment A* to supplement the Manual provided here.

BASIC MATHEMATICS TEST DE

National Foundation for Educational Research
First Published 1969; Standardized 1971–73; Manual Revised 1970
NFER-NELSON, UK
10:05–11:11 (10:05–11:07)
Group
Untimed; (50 mins)
Standard Scores in one-month age bands; some diagnostic use
Consumable booklets

Item Distribution

	Number	Measurement	Space	Algebra	Logic	Statistics
Comprehension	15	7	9	6	12	2
Technique	8	5	–	–	2	–
Recall	–	–	–	–	–	–

Presentation								Response					Context		
Words	Numbers	Algebra	Figures	Graphs	Pictures	Oral		Free Format	Forced Choice	Constructed Lines	Explanation		Abstract	Concrete	Total
40	43	10	18	12	–	–		20	31	4	2		28	27	55

Purposes

This Test is the fourth in a series developed to cover the age range 7–15 years.

'… aims to measure children's understanding of the fundamental relationships and processes which form the basis of all mathematical work. The questions are designed to eliminate as far as possible the effects of different teaching methods …' It is hard to see how this can be done.

'A child's total score on this test gives an indication of his level of mathematical attainment.'

'The standardized score... makes it possible to compare children of different ages within their class or year group who completed the test at the same time.'

'... this test aims to give some diagnostic information about a child's individual strengths and weaknesses.'

Content

Fifty-five items are spread across the following operations: division; multiplication; addition; subtraction; reflection; the interpretation of tabulated data, histograms, an algebraic identity, and a Venn diagram; relations such as equality, equivalence, part-whole relationships, number patterns, ordering, place value; permutations, combinations and probability; sorting; unions and intersections; subsets.

Items consist of clear line drawings separated by solid lines. Most of the test items require quite a high level of reading competence; to this extent the Test will discriminate against poorer readers, no matter what their mathematical competence.

Test development

No data are presented about how the items were developed, nor about any piloting studies which may have been conducted.

3,740 boys and 3,722 girls with a mean age of 11:01 took part in the **standardization** exercise. No information is given about the composition of this sample. Boys outperformed girls by a small but statistically significant amount. The girls in the sample were slightly older than the boys; nevertheless the effect on standardized scores was less than a single point of standard score in favour of the boys. Although this is statistically significant, it has no useful interpretation. The age allowances were not significantly different, so a single conversion table to convert raw scores to standard scores is presented. The Manual explains clearly how the conversion tables are to be used to derive standard scores from raw scores in conjunction with the pupil's age.

304 children (age structure unspecified) provided scripts. These were used to calculate the KR–20 coefficient of **internal consistency** which was found to be 0.96; this corresponds to a value of 3.19 for the standard error of measurement at mean age 11:01. Some indications are provided of the standard error of measurement for pupils whose ages fall at the extremes of the target age range. The way these standard errors of measurement should be interpreted by test users is explained clearly in the Manual.

Information about the **content validity** of the Test can be obtained by inspecting the test items, and the diagnostic grid.

Using the Test

Sensible advice is offered about the **administration** of the Test. For example, the Manual suggests that some useful activity should be devised to give to pupils who finish the Test early. The script for test administration is unambiguous. Children require copies of the test booklet, pencils, and a ruler.

Instructions on **scoring** the Test are clear. In Question 3, the layout of the item on the marking key differs from the layout of items on the Test itself. Since pupils are required to ring correct responses, the different spatial positions might lead to marker error. Marking would have been made simpler if the marking key were exactly the same size as the test booklet, to enable the marker to align pupils' responses exactly with the marking key (as has been done for other tests in this series).

An explanation of the meaning of standard scores is presented in terms of the percentage of children who attain less on the Test than a particular standard score. Each pupil's summary sheet has a space for recording a scoreband, rather than a single score. **Interpretation** of test results is easy. Scores can be compared to those obtained from a large sample: children can be compared to their classmates, with an allowance being made for age differences; test papers can play a diagnostic role in exploring children's misunderstandings (although no advice is given in the Manual about how to use this diagnostic information).

Evaluation

See *Basic Mathematics Test A* for a more general evaluation.

This Test was developed from corresponding tests in the NFER *Mathematics Attainment Test* series, and should be used in preference to tests from that series.

The test items are interesting and attractively presented; the Manual is well laid out, and provides clear instructions about test administration, scoring, and the interpretation of results.

One virtue of the Test is that two questions require pupils to justify their answers. In fact, the justifications which are acceptable are no more than a restatement of the answer, or a very near generalization from it. Nevertheless, since an important mathematical skill is to be able to explain reasons for things, rather than simply to compute them, the inclusion of explanation (even if it is hardly scored at all) within a test of 'basic mathematical attainment' will be a good thing if it stimulates more explanation in mathematics classrooms.

BASIC MATHEMATICS TEST FG

National Foundation for Educational Research
First Published 1969; Standardized 1969 and at other unspecified times; Manual Revised 1971
NFER-NELSON, UK
12:00–15:00 (not clearly stated)
Group Untimed; (no estimate offered)
Three sets of Standard Scores in one-month age bands
Consumable booklets

Item Distribution

	Number	Measurement	Space	Algebra	Logic	Statistics
Comprehension	24	8	10	8	12	3
Technique	8	4	–	–	–	–
Recall	3	–	–	–	–	–

Presentation						
Words	Numbers	Algebra	Figures	Graphs	Pictures	Oral
55	52	15	18	3	–	–

Response			
Free Format	Forced Choice	Constructed Lines	Explanation
30	22	3	–

Context		
Abstract	Concrete	Total
39	16	55

Purposes

'... aims to measure children's understanding of the fundamental relationships and processes which form the basis of all mathematical work. The questions are designed to eliminate as far as possible the effects of different teaching methods, so that the scores from these tests will give a fair basis for comparison.' It is difficult to see how this could be achieved.

'... gives an indication of ... mathematics *attainment*'.

This is the first of the *Basic Mathematics Series* to be produced, which were intended to replace the *Mathematics Attainment Series*. Unlike other tests in the *Basic Mathematics Series*, no attempt is made to describe the blueprint for test construction, nor to offer any diagnostic help based on pupil errors.

Content

Fifty-five items cover: choice of operations to satisfy number equations, calculation of volumes and areas, reading and interpreting tables, binary arithmetic, powers, series, inequalities, equivalent fractions, percentages and decimals, and reflections and rotations. No items deal with algebra, although many require pupils to understand unfamiliar symbols.

Test development

No rationale is offered for the choice of items; no information is given about any piloting that may have taken place. Three separate **standardization** samples are provided. The first is based on 1579 children from 83 secondary schools who took part in the follow-up study of the NFER's Streaming Project in December 1969. No details of the sampling procedure are described. Pupil ages ranged from 12:09 to 13:08. **Reliability** was assessed via KR–21, for the entire sample. The value of 0.95 corresponds to a standard error of measurement (SEM) of 3.2 at mean age 13:02. The second standardization sample is described simply as 'The urban industrial sample.' No further details are given. From the table, we deduce that 3536 children were tested, whose ages ranged from 12:01 to 13:04. Internal consistency was found, via KR–21, to be 0.94, corresponding to an SEM of 3.9. The third sample receives no mention at all in the manual; the conversion table is labelled *Teachers' Score Sheet Project*. The pupil age range is from 13:00 to 15:00; no information is provided about sample size or composition, or reliability.

This information is seriously deficient in its description of the sample composition, and because of the absence of any information concerning sex differences. No advice is offered to users about which conversion table is best suited to their purposes. Standard scores are described as 'provisional' and users are warned to treat the results with caution: 'scores from many more children in a wide variety of areas must be collected and pooled to make the final conversion table ...'

Test **validity** is not discussed.

The Manual relates standard scores to percentiles, to offer an easy interpretation. It also explains how the SEM is to be interpreted.

Using the Test

Little advice is offered about testing practice. Since the Test is untimed, more guidance is needed. The script for test **administration** is sparse, but adequate. Children require copies of the booklet and pencils. Instructions on scoring are clear, and the scoring key is easy to use. One of the response alternatives to Question 36 is wrong. Page totals for right and wrong answers offer some protection against scoring errors. Page totals are transferred to the front of the booklet, summed, and converted to a standard score (which would be better reported as a score band). **Interpretation** of test results is simple. The status of the standardizing samples is unclear, making comparability with notional 'national standards' impossible. Children can, nevertheless, be compared with classmates, making allowances for age differences.

Evaluation

Test items are presented clearly, and cover an interesting range of topics, requiring a grasp of mathematical concepts as well as the exercise of technique. No rationale for test construction is offered. Evidence on standardization is very poor; the manual is seriously deficient in the information provided about the standardizing samples, and even about which tables users should consult. The test Manual is deficient in most other respects too; in 1971 it implied that 'provisional' scores would soon be replaced by properly constructed standard scores (and, hopefully by an improved manual). Users in August 1985 are still offered the same hopes.

It is hard to explain why this should be, since this Test was the first in the *Basic Mathematics Series* to be developed, and covers an age range approximately twice as large as others in the series. One might expect it to be presented in an exemplary way; instead it is very poor, especially in comparison with other *Basic Mathematics* manuals.

Unlike other tests in this series, no attempt is made to diagnose areas of pupil weakness.

BASIC NUMBER DIAGNOSTIC TEST

W.E.C. Gillham
First Published 1980; Standardized
1979
Hodder and Stoughton, UK
5:00–7:00 and older retarded children
(5:00–7:00)
Individual, Oral
Untimed (25 mins)
Number Ages in six-month age
bands; Score Frequencies in six-
month age bands; diagnostic
Consumable booklets

Item Distribution

	Number	Measurement	Space	Algebra	Logic	Statistics
Comprehension	–	–	–	–	–	–
Technique	40	–	–	–	–	–
Recall	10	–	–	–	–	–

Presentation						
Words	Numbers	Algebra	Figures	Graphs	Pictures	Oral
50	50	–	14	–	–	50

Response			
Free Format	Forced Choice	Constructed Lines	Explanation
50	–	6	–

Context		
Abstract	Concrete	Total
20	30	50

Purposes

'The test assesses number performance or *skills* and, by careful observation of the way the child sets about the test items, and in particular by noting what errors he makes and *how* he goes wrong, it is possible to gain insight into his thinking and his strategies, i.e. the ways in which he deals with the items. This points the way to remediation.'

'... intended for *individual* use, by teachers or educational psychologists, with children in the age-range five to seven years, or with older children who are retarded in their number skills.'

'Its main purpose is to show what a child can do (and cannot do) so that specific teaching objectives for that individual child can be determined. It is, therefore, *content–* or *criterion–* referenced rather than norm-referenced.'

'... to complement the *Basic Number Screening Test* and the *Leicester Number Test...*'

The Test is intended to be given at regular intervals '... so that a child's progress can be charted and ... teaching requirements revised.'

The test is intended to cover 'the basic number skills that a child could reasonably be expected to have mastered by the age of seven years.'

'Because the test sets out to assess for teaching, the content represents a basic *curriculum* ... though far from being a complete curriculum.'

Content

Fifty items require pupils to recite; name and copy numbers; to write numbers in sequence and to dictation; to count and select bricks; to add and subtract objects represented in drawings; and to add and subtract numerals. Items are presented in a booklet which pupil and tester share; test items and retest items both appear in the same booklet. Items are presented roughly in order of difficulty, with similar activities grouped together.

Test development

There is no description of how the items were developed, how they relate to each other, or of any theory of number acquisition which might underlie the Test. We learn only that the Test 'is the outcome of eighteen months' continuous revision.'

The Test was **standardized** in the Spring Term of 1979, 'in a representative sample of primary and infant schools in the City of

Nottingham and the Rutland area of Leicestershire.' The word 'standardized' seems too grand. Scores from 292 pupils whose ages were within six weeks of six-month age boundaries from 5:00 to 7:00 were collected. Of these, 82 were pupils aged 7:00 with a median score of 47 (out of a possible 50). Score frequencies are presented within five-point score bands for each six-month age group. Overall, test scores appear to be bimodal; this might simply be a product of the small sample size, but certainly reflects its inadequacy. A second table offers 'Number Ages' for different scores. Again, these offer guidance of only the crudest kind, because of the size of the sample, and the dramatic increases in scores with age. For example, median scores at different ages were 5:00 (13); 5:06 (33); 6:00 (43); 6:06 (43); 7:00 (48). These hardly reflect a smooth progression.

Normative scores are not necessarily a useful aspect of diagnostic tests; descriptions of likely errors (with approximate relative frequencies), together with possible misconceptions about number and suggestions for remediation, are far more important. No serious attempt has been made to offer such descriptions.

Reliability was calculated for a sample of 32 children using test-retest items where available, and alternative items where not. The value for Spearman's *rho* of 0.93 was taken as evidence that 'the test is satisfactorily reliable.' This conclusion is not warranted by the data.

The absence of any **validation** studies is lamentable; no evidence is offered on either construct validation or validity against educational criteria.

Using the Test

Instructions and details of **administration** are incorporated into the Test, to avoid the need for continual reference to the Manual. Instructions may be modified when it seems appropriate, but users are warned that deviations are likely to invalidate any comparisons with test norms. No guidance is given about how pupils should be introduced to the Test.

The Test requires an ordinary pencil, a red pencil and 30 small plastic bricks. Pupil and tester share the booklet, which is printed so that they sit at right angles to each other. The Tester records all the pupil's responses, including errors, but defers scoring until the Test is complete. Attention is to be focused on the nature of failures, and to gain understanding of how and why a pupil is going wrong. An understanding of processes which lead to *correct* solutions might lead to suggestions for remediation if they are inefficient, or likely to be error-prone. The script for administration is clear.

The procedure for **scoring** is clear; no scoring key is provided, presumably because testers are expected to reflect upon each item, rather than focus on total score. The Manual offers clear guidance on marking, and a few bland comments on remediation. For the purpose of **interpretation**, scores are then transferred to the front of the booklet, and a bar chart of scores under different headings is constructed. Two sorts of teaching objectives can then be identified. Medium-term objectives are to focus on those tasks which the pupil was unsure of, or achieved some partial success in; longer term objectives are to increase scores by five points in each behavioural category assessed.

Evaluation

How can we account for, and remedy, the poor performance of pupils who fail to make much progress in basic number work? A sensible start is to consider some of the component skills, to look for deficiencies, and to offer specific remediation (one might also look for larger misconceptions, and try to remedy them). This process obviously requires a structured interview with the individual child. This Test attempts to provide a vehicle for such an interview.

One might reasonably expect a 'basic number diagnostic test' to offer an account of the acquisition of number, a description of observed patterns of pupil errors, hypotheses about their associated misconceptions and some clear suggestions for remediation. None of these are present. The Test also avoids any consideration of the deployment of number skills, such as questions involving the choice of operation. Standardizing data are quite inadequate. The Test relies heavily on skilful use and interpretation by the tester, with a little guidance from the Manual. It is not at all clear that an experienced teacher would be any better off with this test than with an interview based on any other collection of items from infant mathematics books, or that a novice would get much help at all from it.

BASIC NUMBER SCREENING TEST

W.E.C. Gillham and K. Hesse
First Published 1976; Standardized 1976
Hodder and Stoughton, UK
7:00–12:00 (7:06–11:06) and older retarded children
Group, Oral
Untimed; (35 mins)
Raw Scores; Number Age in three-month age bands
Consumable booklets

Item Distribution

	Number	Measurement	Space	Algebra	Logic	Statistics
Comprehension	8	–	–	–	1	–
Technique	20	–	–	–	–	–
Recall	2	–	–	–	–	–

Presentation						
Words	Numbers	Algebra	Figures	Graphs	Pictures	Oral
14	30	–	5	–	–	14

Response			
Free Format	Forced Choice	Constructed Lines	Explanation
25	1	4	–

Context		
Abstract	Concrete	Total
24	6	30

Purposes

'The main purpose of the present test is to help identify the child whose number attainments are low for his age or who is failing to make continued progress. It does not show *how* or *why* the child is failing, but directs attention to those children whose difficulties need to be explored individually and in detail.'

'... to give a quick assessment of a child's understanding of the basic principles underlying the number system (number concepts) and the processes involved in computation (number skills).'

'... provides an *approximate* classification of attainment.'

'... of value both as a group screening test and as an individual test ... where a broad classification is adequate. Where a more detailed classification is required ... *Leicester* and *Nottingham Number Tests*, being longer and related to specific age levels, are more appropriate.'

Content

Thirty items cover the use of: counting, addition, subtraction, multiplication, division, fractions, place value, series and decimals, mainly in the form of conventional sums or number sentences. Two parallel forms of the Test are available.

Test development

The Manual reports that 'The content of the test has been determined by our understanding of the development of children's number concepts, an appreciation of the changing nature of mathematics in schools, ...' These assertions are unwarranted – the test contents are banal, and show no appreciation of the changing nature of mathematics in schools. It is hard to imagine how they can be related to the development of children's number concepts.

The Test was **standardized** on a sample of 3042 children in the city area of Nottingham, which was used previously 'for the standardization of the *Leicester* and *Nottingham Number Tests*, where the norms obtained had been found satisfactory.' It is hard to know what this remark means. This standardization sample is somewhat small; it is also clear that no attempt has been made to test a representative sample of the seven– to 12–year-old school population.

'Test scores are converted into Number Ages, which represent the average performance of children at the various age levels.

Age norms are seen as the most meaningful way of expressing scores on a wide-ranging test such as the present one, despite their technical limitations.'

These Number Age norms consist of a column of raw scores, together with a column of Number Ages (in three-month steps). Each three-month step corresponds to one (or occasionally two) raw score points.

No information is provided about the number of children tested in each age band; nor have we any idea about the standard error of measurement. The Manual explicitly states that Number Age for ages beyond 11:06 and below 7:06 are obtained by extrapolation.

No information is provided about the relative performances of girls and boys, either overall, or at different ages.

The Manual asserts that 'a very realistic estimate of reliability' was obtained by correlating scores of the two forms of the Test, administered one week apart. The resulting correlation was found to be 0.93. Such information on **reliability** is of little use since we have no idea either about the number of children involved nor about the age-range, nor about the spread of ability.

'Since the Test directly samples the attainments it is measuring ... validity is assumed not to be a serious problem.' In one school the authors asked teachers to rate children on a seven-point scale before the Test was administered. These ratings (presumably about the number skills of the children) were then correlated with subsequent test scores. The correlation (Spearman's *rho*) averaged 0.82: 'very satisfactory for this type of measure'.

These **validity** data are also questionable. Again, we have no information about the number of children, the number of teachers, or the age or ability spread of the children. Bland assertions about 'very satisfactory' are of little use.

Using the test

The introduction to test **administration** offers sound guidance. Two parallel forms of Test are provided so that children can be re-tested. The instructions for both forms of the Test are identical, as is the scoring. The authors assert that both forms of the Tests can be used at the same time to ease problems of class administration.

'The test is untimed, putting much responsibility on the judgement and sensitivity of the teacher who gives it ... The guiding principle is to avoid causing unnecessary anxiety by hurrying, to allow just enough time for those children who are clearly capable of writing an answer.'

Two versions of administration instructions are available, one for group administration, and the other for individual administration. Sensibly, the Manual suggests that for all the children the first few items can be gone through quickly; and that children in the younger age-range can stop part-way through the test, since their chances of picking up marks in the later stages is slight. Pupils require a copy of the test booklet, and pencils.

The examiner's script is clear enough. The script for the administration of each item is also quite adequate. The instructions for **marking** are quite clear. Mirror reversals are accepted; errors of reverse order (for example, 32 when the correct answer is 23) are acceptable on the early test items (which might characterize correct responses by rather younger children), and are unacceptable in the later part of the Test. The scoring key is adequate, although it cannot be lined up exactly with the test script itself. Separate totals for right and wrong answers would be a useful addition to the test form, to guard against marker errors.

In Item M on Form B, the response box for the mark is missing; scorers should be made aware of this fact, and it should be changed in future versions of the Test.

Interpretation involves using the raw score to look up the Number Age of each pupil. No data are provided about t'.e standard error of measurement (which is likely to be high) ar.d the inexperienced user may mistakenly believe the Test to be accurate to within a few months of 'Number Age'. The results are likely to have significance only in the cases of pupils whose Number Age is markedly below their chronological age.

Evaluation

The Test sets out to be a simple screening test on number ability. For the most part, items are constrained to constructed responses to conventional arithmetic problems. Little attempt is made to look at the child's ability to deploy these basic number skills – for example in choosing which operations to use. Just 30 items are used to judge the number skills of pupils whose ages ranged from seven to 12 years. This is a rather small set of items to do anything other than the coarsest of screening.

The Manual is inadequate in a number of important respects: notably in its description of the standardizing sample; reliability data; validity; and the presentation of norms as Number Ages, with no comments on measurement error. These inadequacies are dealt with by rather cavalier remarks in the Manual, such as 'very satisfactory' and 'very realistic estimate' and the like. Such comments are of no use to teachers who are likely to use the Test, and provide no encouragement for test users to learn more about the principles and process of test development.

It is hard to imagine a sensible use for this Test, other than to provide an extremely crude screening for the identification of children who are under-performing quite dramatically in relation to Nottingham schoolchildren.

BRISTOL ACHIEVEMENT TESTS

Alan Brimer
First Published 1969; Standardization
date not stated; Revised 1982
NFER-NELSON, UK
Junior:
  Second year (Level 1) 8:00–9:11
  (8:09–9:08)
  Third Year (Level 2) 9:00–10:11
  (9:09–10:08)
  Fourth Year (Level 3) 10:00–11:11
  (10:09–11:08)
Secondary:
  First Year (Level 4) 11:00–12:11
  (11:09–12:08)
  Second Year (Level 5) 12:00–
  13:11 (12:09–13:08)
Group
Timed; 55 mins
Standard Scores in two-month age
bands; Deciles and Percentiles; Pupil
Profiles
Consumable booklets

LEVEL I
Item Distribution

	Number	Measurement	Space	Algebra	Logic	Statistics
Comprehension	15	16	15	–	20	–
Technique	33	1	–	–	1	–
Recall	–	8	–	–	–	–

Presentation						
Words	Numbers	Algebra	Figures	Graphs	Pictures	Oral
80	80	–	60	–	–	–

Response			
Free Format	Forced Choice	Constructed Lines	Explanation
52	43	–	–

Context		
Abstract	Concrete	Total
65	30	95

LEVEL 2
Item Distribution

	Number	Measurement	Space	Algebra	Logic	Statistics
Comprehension	27	14	15	–	14	–
Technique	44	2	–	–	6	–
Recall	–	10	–	–	–	–

Presentation

Words	Numbers	Algebra	Figures	Graphs	Pictures	Oral
85	81	–	61	–	–	–

Response

Free Format	Forced Choice	Constructed Lines	Explanation
55	45	–	–

Context

Abstract	Concrete	Total
30	70	100

LEVEL 3
Item Distribution

	Number	Measurement	Space	Algebra	Logic	Statistics
Comprehension	33	28	16	–	17	–
Technique	31	1	–	–	7	–
Recall	–	–	–	–	–	–

Presentation

Words	Numbers	Algebra	Figures	Graphs	Pictures	Oral
97	86	–	61	7	–	–

Response

Free Format	Forced Choice	Constructed Lines	Explanation
57	40	30	–

Context

Abstract	Concrete	Total
20	80	100

LEVEL 4
Item Distribution

	Number	Measurement	Space	Algebra	Logic	Statistics
Comprehension	37	25	24	–	16	–
Technique	22	5	–	–	2	–
Recall	8	–	6	–	–	–

Presentation						
Words	Numbers	Algebra	Figures	Graphs	Pictures	Oral
100	77	–	75	–	–	–

Response			
Free Format	Forced Choice	Constructed Lines	Explanation
46	54	–	–

Context		
Abstract	Concrete	Total
23	77	100

LEVEL 5
Item Distribution

	Number	Measurement	Space	Algebra	Logic	Statistics
Comprehension	53	9	15	–	34	4
Technique	11	4	–	3	–	–
Recall	2	–	7	–	–	–

Presentation						
Words	Numbers	Algebra	Figures	Graphs	Pictures	Oral
100	96	8	50	10	–	–

Response			
Free Format	Forced Choice	Constructed Lines	Explanation
68	32	–	–

Context		
Abstract	Concrete	Total
19	81	100

Purposes

'The *Bristol Achievement Tests* have been constructed together and matched to produce balanced measures of basic skills and concepts in school achievement.'

'... the tests focus deliberately on skills and conceptual strategies of knowing rather than upon the content of knowledge ... they favour the diagnosis of individual difficulties which might otherwise escape the teacher's scrutiny and ... suggest ways in which teaching might be directed to secure greater competence.'

'... can be used as a form of diagnosis of the particular difficulties of a child, or in terms of the particular strengths or weaknesses present in the curriculum.'

'The profile sheets are likely to be used ... as part of a cumulative school record for a child and also for ... sorting children into groups. They are a more convenient way of ensuring that mixed achievement level groups are formed into classes since they summarize the levels of achievement in more than one area of the curriculum.'

'A class teacher ... may wish to know for a particular child whether his performance is as excellent or as low as he believes it to be ... He may also wish to compare the performance of children in his own class with those of other classes in the same school.'

Content

The *Bristol Achievement Tests* assess performance in English, Mathematics and Study Skills, at each of five levels. Only the Mathematics test will be reviewed here. At each level, the Test comprises five subtests which are administered in the same session, and timed separately. Parallel forms of each test are available. Subtests focus on number, reasoning, space, measurement, arithmetic laws and conventions.

Tests of number include matching dots, directed number problems, binary arithmetic. Tests of reasoning include Venn diagrams, strings of shapes, word reasoning problems, probability and ratio. Tests of spatial reasoning include problems involving cut-up shapes, bearings and distances, knowledge of geometry. Test of measurement include conversion of units, reading tables, planning areas, the use of graphical information. Tests of arithmetic laws and conventions include; sums, choice of operation, identities.

Test development

'... the theoretical basis for the sampling of achievement was the product of an investigation of the psychological, pedagogical and curriculum literature. ... No claim is made to an identification of the fundamental elements of skill and conceptual strategy within each subject.'

'... throughout the levels a developmental framework is being followed and a range of developmental stages is encompassed within each level.'

Curriculum sampling involved the identification of content and processes; this was followed by attempts to write items to operationalize these constructs, and to represent the necessary age and development levels. One thousand items were evaluated during the first trials, which involved 4,863 pupils; 848 of these items had appropriate statistical properties. Trial forms were administered to samples of about 100 children at each level, before the main standardization exercise.

The **standardization** was based on a national sample; schools in England and Wales were selected so as to be representative in terms of size, type and urban-rural character. Data from 5,779 pupils are reported. Data show quite large, and statistically significant differences in scores between girls and boys at Levels 2 (form A), 3 (forms A and B) and 5 (forms A and B); nevertheless common norms are provided. The date of standardization is not stated.

'Age norms were produced over a twenty-four month period so that the variation in age within a level would be catered for by the test at any point in the education year in which testing took place.' It is not clear how this could be accomplished given the way that pupils were sampled. Norms for pupils aged 8:00 to 9:08 and 13:09 to 13:11 are extrapolated.

To explore **reliability**, parallel forms of each Test were administered to samples of about 1000 children at each level, within a two week period. Values for the whole Test ranged from $r = 0.92$ to $r = 0.94$; and for subtests from $r = 0.63$ to $r = 0.89$. These correspond to a standard error of measurement which ranges for the whole test from 4.19 to 3.67, and for subtests from 9.39 to 5.03 units of standard score.

Scores on Form B are higher than scores on Form A (which should always be given first) and separate norms are provided. Somewhat surprisingly, for Level 4 (age range 11:00 to 12:11) 'no significant increase of score with age occurred, and therefore no age adjustment was required in the table'. A similar pattern was found for English at Level 5, but nowhere else. No explanations are offered for these odd results.

Content **validity** is referred to as 'rational validity'. The Manual claims 'rational validity' without describing test content in any detail: '... statistical data is only partly available at the time of publication ... More is needed in the form of correlations with external criteria ... It was judged better not to delay publication and it is intended that such data will be added to this manual as it becomes available.' That was written in 1969.

The correlations between each Test and every other Test at every level suggest that a large common factor underlies the performances on all tests (including those of English and Study Skills).

Using the Test

Pupils require pencils and copies of the test booklet; the test administrator needs some method for accurate timing. If the Test is given to more than 30 children, an assistant should be present. Details of the **administration** are rather brief. The invigilator must instruct pupils to move onto different subtests at specified times; instructions should include writing down these times. No script is provided to introduce or explain the Tests to pupils.

Pupils take Tests at a level which reflects both their ages and length of schooling. Parallel forms of each test at all levels are available. Pupils are advised to 'Work fast. Write if you can, rather than print.'

A **scoring key** is provided, which aligns exactly with the test booklet, to facilitate scoring; markers' discretion in scoring is described. Scores are totalled on each page, but no other provision is made to avoid scorer errors.

Pupil profile sheets are available, which offer a summary of a child's performance in different domains with respect to the standardization sample; the user is directed to record bands, which incorporate the standard error of measurement, rather than just the score, in order to avoid the over-interpretation of small differences of score. 'Expected scores' are also derived with no justification, from each child's vocabulary score. The derivation of profiles is based on percentiles and deciles, for no obvious reason, and at the cost of some rounding. Derivation could have been based on standard scores, and the same display coded to allow easy interpretation in terms of percentiles.

The **interpretation** of standard scores, deciles and percentiles is explained; in addition, the Manual has one section devoted to 'The Principles of Mental Measurement', and another entitled 'The Standard Error of Measurement'. Guidance is also offered on how an appropriate measure of error can be derived in order to judge differences observed on pupil profiles. This guidance was not followed in the example, which illustrates the interpretation of profiles. Users are advised, in general, to use score bands two error units wide 'where the consequences of the educational decision are positive action towards the child' and to use bands four units wide where 'on balance, disadvantage to the child when one is wrong is comparable with the positive advantage when one is right.'

Individual profiles should be judged against the whole school profile (which may deviate from the standardization sample), as well as against the standardization sample.

'The purpose of these sub-test scores is not to suggest what kind of attention should be given but rather that a case for further study has been made out and that an appropriate diagnostic test might reveal where teaching could be more profitably placed.'

Evaluation

The Test claims to be based on a study of modern curriculae (modern in 1969) and theories of psychology and education. A description of these studies, relating them to the rules for item construction, would have been helpful in assessing the construct validity of the Test, and in offering hints about possible remedial teaching. Test items are well presented and offer some interesting intellectual challenges; nevertheless one might question the presence of 15 items devoted to binary arithmetic, out of 100 items on Level 5. Questions 11 to 20 refer to the use of paper tape readers on computers; Form A has three questions on algebraic identities, and Form B has none; some questions use rather odd notations for recurring decimals and powers, which pupils are supposed to be familiar with. In all the subtests, the distinctness of each one is rather doubtful.

Test standardization also revealed oddities; there were no score increases with age on some tests; sex differences were quite large, but ignored in the preparation of norms; test-retest of parallel forms was the only form of reporting reliability. No year of standardization is given, let alone *month*.

The process of profiling seems unnecessarily cumbersome, being based on percentiles rather than standard scores. When subtests are highly correlated, as they are here, profiles are unlikely to be very informative. As the Manual warns us, it is easy to over-interpret differences in subtest scores; nevertheless, it commits just this error when illustrating the use of profiles.

There are no suggestions about how test scores might be used; this is a pity, given that test development was based on a detailed analysis of cognitive development and current curricula. The Manual is extensive, but rather turgidly written.

CHELSEA DIAGNOSTIC MATHEMATICS TESTS

Kathleen Hart, Margaret Brown, Daphne Kerslake, Dietmar Küchemann,
Graham Ruddock
First Published: Tests, 1984; Manual, 1985
NFER-NELSON, UK

Algebra	12 + to 15+ (12+ to 15+); Untimed (40 mins)
Fractions 1	11 + to 13+ (11+ to 13+); Untimed (30 mins)
Fractions 2	13 + to 15+ (13+ to 15+); Untimed (30 mins)
Graphs	12 + to 15+ (12+ to 15+); Untimed (45 mins)
Measurement	11 + to 14+ (11+ to 14+); Untimed (60 mins)
Number Operations	9 + to 15+ (10+ to 13+); Untimed (40 mins)
Place Value and Decimals	11 + to 15+ (11+ to 15+); Untimed (60 mins)
Ratio and Proportion	12 + to 15+ (12+ to 15+); Untimed (40 mins)
Reflection and Rotation	12 + to 15+ (12+ to 15+); Untimed (60 mins)
Vectors	13 + to 15+ (13+ to 15+); Untimed (60 mins)

Group
Levels of understanding;
diagnostic
Consumable booklets

ALGEBRA
Item Distribution

	Number	Measurement	Space	Algebra	Logic	Statistics
Comprehension	–	–	4	12	–	–
Technique	–	–	6	16	–	–
Recall	–	–	–	–	–	–

Presentation						
Words	Numbers	Algebra	Figures	Graphs	Pictures	Oral
28	25	27	10	–	–	–

Response			
Free Format	Forced Choice	Constructed Lines	Explanation
30	1	–	10

Context		
Abstract	Concrete	Total
17	13	30

Note: these tables refer only to items which are used in the calculation of pupils' levels of understanding; 51 items are presented in the test booklet.

FRACTIONS I
Item Distribution

	Number	Measurement	Space	Algebra	Logic	Statistics
Comprehension	12	–	2	–	–	–
Technique	16	–	–	–	–	–
Recall	–	–	–	–	–	–

Presentation						
Words	Numbers	Algebra	Figures	Graphs	Pictures	Oral
28	28	–	11	–	–	–

Response			
Free Format	Forced Choice	Constructed Lines	Explanation
28	1	6	1

Context		
Abstract	Concrete	Total
8	20	28

Note: these tables refer only to items which are used in the calculation of pupils' levels of understanding; 45 items are presented in the test booklet, together with an 18–item test of computational skill.

FRACTIONS 2
Item Distribution

	Number	Measurement	Space	Algebra	Logic	Statistics
Comprehension	14	–	3	1	–	–
Technique	12	–	–	–	–	–
Recall	–	–	–	–	–	–

Presentation						
Words	Numbers	Algebra	Figures	Graphs	Pictures	Oral
26	25	1	8	–	–	–

Response			
Free Format	Forced Choice	Constructed Lines	Explanation
23	3	1	1

Context		
Abstract	Concrete	Total
9	17	26

Note: these tables refer only to items which are used in the calculation of pupils' levels of understanding; 47 items are presented in the test booklet, together with a 20–item test of computational skill.

GRAPHS
Item Distribution

	Number	Measurement	Space	Algebra	Logic	Statistics
Comprehension	17	–	–	–	4	–
Technique	7	–	–	–	–	–
Recall	–	–	–	–	–	–

Presentation						
Words	Numbers	Algebra	Figures	Graphs	Pictures	Oral
24	24	13	–	24	–	–

Response			
Free Format	Forced Choice	Constructed Lines	Explanation
22	2	8	2

Context		
Abstract	Concrete	Total
0	24	24

Note: these tables refer only to items which are used in the calculation of pupils' levels of understanding; 54 items are presented in the test booklet.

MEASUREMENT
Item Distribution

	Number	Measurement	Space	Algebra	Logic	Statistics
Comprehension	–	8	23	–	–	–
Technique	–	–	2	–	–	–
Recall	–	–	–	–	–	–

Presentation						
Words	Numbers	Algebra	Figures	Graphs	Pictures	Oral
25	25	–	25	–	1	–

Response			
Free Format	Forced Choice	Constructed Lines	Explanation
21	4	–	–

Context		
Abstract	Concrete	Total
0	25	25

Note: these tables refer only to items which are used in the calculation of pupils' levels of understanding; 41 items are presented in the test booklet.

NUMBER
OPERATIONS
Item Distribution

	Number	Measurement	Space	Algebra	Logic	Statistics
Comprehension	14	–	–	–	–	–
Technique	–	–	–	–	–	–
Recall	–	–	–	–	–	–

Presentation

Words	Numbers	Algebra	Figures	Graphs	Pictures	Oral
14	14	–	1	–	8	9

Response

Free Format	Forced Choice	Constructed Lines	Explanation
5	9	–	5

Context

Abstract	Concrete	Total
0	14	14

PLACE-VALUE AND
DECIMALS
Item Distribution

	Number	Measurement	Space	Algebra	Logic	Statistics
Comprehension	7	–	–	–	–	–
Technique	27	4	3	–	–	–
Recall	4	–	–	–	–	–

Presentation						
Words	Numbers	Algebra	Figures	Graphs	Pictures	Oral
38	39	0	8	–	1	–

Response			
Free Format	Forced Choice	Constructed Lines	Explanation
31	8	0	0

Context		
Abstract	Concrete	Total
30	9	39

Note: these tables refer only to items which are used in the calculation of pupils' levels of understanding; 73 items are presented in the test booklet.

RATIO AND
PROPORTION
Item Distribution

	Number	Measurement	Space	Algebra	Logic	Statistics
Comprehension	20	2	–	–	–	–
Technique	–	–	–	–	–	–
Recall	–	–	–	–	–	–

Presentation						
	Numbers	Algebra	Figures	Graphs	Pictures	Oral
20	20	–	12	–	–	–

Response			
Free Format	Forced Choice	Constructed Lines	Explanation
20	–	–	–

Context		
Abstract	Concrete	Total
–	20	20

Note: these tables refer only to items which are used in the calculation of pupils' levels of understanding; 25 items are presented in the test booklet.

REFLECTION AND
ROTATION
Item Distribution

	Number	Measurement	Space	Algebra	Logic	Statistics
Comprehension	–	8	40	–	–	–
Technique	–	–	1	–	–	–
Recall	–	–	–	–	–	–

Presentation						
Words	Numbers	Algebra	Figures	Graphs	Pictures	Oral
41	9	–	41	–	–	–

Response			
Free Format	Forced Choice	Constructed Lines	Explanation
40	1	32	2

Context		
Abstract	Concrete	Total
–	41	41

Note: these tables refer only to items which are used in the calculation of pupils' levels of understanding; 57 items are presented in the test booklet.

VECTORS
Item Distribution

	Number	Measurement	Space	Algebra	Logic	Statistics
Comprehension	15	31	39	5	–	–
Technique	3	–	–	2	–	–
Recall	–	–	–	–	–	–

Presentation						
Words	Numbers	Algebra	Figures	Graphs	Pictures	Oral
53	30	26	37	–	–	–

Response			
Free Format	Forced Choice	Constructed Lines	Explanation
48	5	3	10

Context		
Abstract	Concrete	Total
9	44	53

Note: these tables refer only to items which are used in the calculation of pupils' levels of understanding; 76 items are presented in the test booklet.

Purposes

The Tests arose from the *Concepts in Secondary Mathematics and Science (CSMS)* research programme, carried out at Chelsea College, University of London, between 1974–79.

'The aim of the mathematics project was to identify a developmental hierarchy of understanding connecting the mathematical concepts commonly taught in secondary school, in order to provide a structure which would help teachers and curriculum designers to plan appropriate teaching materials, and to match them to individual children.'

The CSMS mathematics research adopted a Piagetian framework. The *Chelsea Diagnostic Mathematics Tests* do not, however, assume that intellectual development is rigidly tied to chronological age, or that stages of development progress inexorably, or that cognitive development is broadly the same across tasks and contexts, as some critics say Piaget does!

'Assessment of any sort should be carried out for a definite purpose. A worthwhile reason for testing children is a teacher's desire to tailor his or her teaching more closely to what the child knows and what he seems ... able to do. The questions in the *Chelsea Diagnostic Mathematics Tests* have been shown to be useful both in interviews and as written tests.'

'The tests are diagnostic instruments designed to be used either before or after a substantial amount of the topic is presented. Used before the teaching, the results should provide a guide to the present level of understanding of each child, enabling the teacher to match the child's work to what the child knows. After the topic has been taught, the tests can be used in a similar way to assess the degree of understanding displayed by individual children.'

'The marking schemes for each test enable the teacher to assign a child to a "level of understanding" for that topic ... This is preferable to compiling just a total test "score", as it will show the teacher the type of item at which the pupil is unsuccessful (the level(s) not attained), besides what he appears to understand (the level(s) attained).'

'The descriptions of the levels of each test ... refer both to the mathematical ideas involved and to the methods used by children to solve that group of items.'

The purpose of each of the 10 Tests is to provide an assessment of a child's 'level of understanding' on some key topic area in mathematics. Each Test also provides a good deal of information about systematic misunderstandings in each domain. Given this information, teachers should be in a stronger position to plan future teaching (for example, by remediating misconceptions; by focusing on the next level of understanding). Some data are presented which allow comparison with a larger sample in terms of error rates on individual questions, and in terms of the proportion of pupils classified at different levels of understanding; nevertheless, the primary function of each Test is diagnosis, not normative comparison.

Content

The Chelsea Diagnostic Mathematics Tests are a collection of ten Tests, each focused on a single topic in secondary mathematics. Their uses are covered by a single *Teacher's Guide*.

'The objective of the Algebra test is to assess children's levels of understanding across a broad range of typical secondary school algebra tasks. These include substitution, simplifying expressions, and constructing, interpreting and solving equations. The assessment focuses on the different ways in which children use and interpret the letters in generalized arithmetic ... an attempt has been made to minimise the need for remembered techniques and conventions.'

'The questions in *Fractions 1* involve the conventions used in the labelling of fractions and the operations of addition and subtraction. The test was designed for first– and second–year secondary pupils; the operations of multiplication and division appear in ... *Fractions 2* ...'

Fractions 1 has a supplement, *Fractions 1 (Computation)* where computations involving fractions mirror the ones set in the main test.

'The questions in *Fractions 2* involve the conventions used in the labelling of fractions and the operations of addition, subtraction, multiplication and division. The test was designed for third– and fourth– year secondary pupils ...'

Fractions 2 has a supplement, *Fractions 2 (Computation)*, where calculations involving fractions mirror the ones set in the main Test.

'The objective of the *Graphs* test is to assess the student's conceptual understanding of the basic ideas of graphs, namely bar charts, co-ordinates, scale, continuous graphs and simple equations.'

'The aim of the *Measurement* test is to assess the level of understanding within the topics of Length, Area and Volume ...'

Some of the questions have been adapted from Piagetian tasks, but are presented exclusively in paper and pencil format.

'The aim of the *Number Operations* test is to assess conceptual understanding of the four basic number operations ... when applied to whole numbers.'

The Test is in two parts; the first part describes situations and requires pupils to choose sums which match these situations; the second part presents sums and invites pupils to compose an appropriate story (for example, for '9+3', one might reply 'I had nine marbles, then won three more').

'The approach is ... to find out whether children can both recognize straightforward instances in which each operation applies, and also provide for themselves a concrete example for each operation. The test does *not* aim to assess skill at mechanical computation...'

Unlike other tests in the series, it does not provide an assessment of a child's level of understanding; rather it

'was designed mainly to indicate the extent to which children had acquired sufficient understanding of the meaning of the four number operations to form a basis for many of the topics in the secondary mathematics curriculum'.

'The purpose of the *Place-Value and Decimals* test is to assess whether children can meaningfully use the base ten place-value notation for both whole numbers and decimals, in the sense of both understanding how it works and applying it to appropriate situations.'

The *Ratio and Proportion* Test does not include the manipulation of fractions (which is the focus of other tests), nor is knowledge of technical terms (including 'ratio' and 'proportion') required.

'The objective of the *Reflection and Rotation* test is to assess children's understanding of these two principal transformations of the plane ... an attempt has been made to minimise the need for remembered techniques and conventions ... The test is in three parts: single reflections, single rotations ... and combinations of reflections and rotations.'

The *Vectors* test will 'assess the level of understanding within the topic of Vectors reached by an individual child'. The Test is divided into four sections: a) where vectors are ordered n-tuples that *do not* represent movements or positions; b) where vectors are ordered n–tuples that *do* represent movements and positions; c) where free vectors are presented, with appropriate notation (for example, *a*); d) where route vectors are presented (for example, $\overrightarrow{AB}$).

Test development

The Tests grew out of the *CSMS* project, which set out to establish, within each mathematical topic, a hierarchy of difficulty levels which would correspond to 'levels of understanding'. Since the focus is on understanding, relatively few items are devoted to routine technical skills. Several questions were adapted from those used by Piaget and his co-workers; a bibliography offers pointers to the links between *CSMS* and the Genevan school, and to detailed descriptions of the *CSMS* research project.

The research underwent four phases: item design; individual interviews; large-scale testing; and statistical analysis. The concepts underlying each item are described in the Manual. On each topic, interviews were held with about 30 pupils, based around a selection of test items. Items 'which appeared to provide information on understanding, were incorporated in a class test format.' Items were modified during trials; interviews provided information on both correct and incorrect solution strategies used by children. Incorrect strategies that consistently produced the same wrong responses were noted, and are coded as part of the scoring of the paper and pencil tests.

'The tests which have been published are essentially those used in the paper and pencil surveys, which took place mainly in 1976 and 1977. The facility values which are quoted for ... questions are those which resulted from the subsequent analyses. The interviews which had preceded the surveys enabled the researchers to code with some insight specific errors occurring in the wide-scale testing, and to suggest reasons for both correct and incorrect answers. Details of these have been given in the individual entries for each test...'

In all, 13,477 pupils took part in the *CSMS* mathematics trials, based in 189 schools. Testing took place mainly during the summers of 1976 and 1977.

'The schools used for the large-scale testing were of different types drawn from urban and rural areas in England. The population in each year group for each test matched the distribution for the total population of British school children at the NFER *Non-Verbal Test DH*.'

Test DH is suitable for children aged 11 to 13. Schools gave the Test to their second years (age 12 to 13 years); if school staff were confident that pupils in the third and fourth years came from the same catchment area as the second-year pupils, and were selected for entry on the same criteria, the distribution of second-year scores was assumed to hold for the other years, too. If not, then only second-year pupils were tested. The numbers of children and schools who took part in each survey are shown in Table 1.

'The hierarchies of understanding, by the very nature of their formulation, are dependent upon items which appear in each of the ten tests. No claim is made as to their uniqueness, but the demands of each level should assist teachers in planning the development of their schemes of work.'

A hierarchy of levels of understanding should have all the following properties:

Table 1: The numbers of children and schools involved in the CSMS Mathematics Trials

Test	Date of Testing	Year group				
		4th (Junior) 10+ to 11+	1st 11+ to 12+	2nd 12+ to 13+	3rd 13+ to 14+	4th 14+ to 15+
Algebra	1976			1,128 (8)	961 (7)	731 (7)
Fractions 1	1977		246 (6)	309 (9)		
Fractions 2	1977				308 (6)	215 (6)
Graphs	1976			389 (6)	594 (6)	413 (5)
Measurement	1977		169 (5)	444 (8)	373 (8)	
Number Operations	1975	497 (7)	247 (4)	130 (2)		
Place-Value and Decimals	1977		170 (5)	294 (8)	247 (7)	239 (7)
Ratio and Proportion	1976			800 (8)	767 (6)	690 (7)
Reflection and Rotation	1977			293 (9)	449 (8)	284 (6)
Vectors	1976				1,140 (9)	950 (9)

Note: The figures in brackets show the number of schools from which each sample was drawn.

1. Items within (and to some extent between) levels should measure similar things;
2. Items higher in the hierarchy should be harder than items at lower levels;
3. Pupils who pass items at high levels should also pass items at lower levels;
4. Levels should be distinct.

Property 2 can be satisfied easily by examining item facilities. Property 1 can be examined via a measure of homogeneity; the *phi* coefficient was used for this study. Property 3 can be examined by calculating Loevinger's H between each pair of items, and by ensuring that the values are adequately high.

Pupils were judged to have attained a particular level of understanding when they completed two-thirds of the items at that level successfully, together with similar passes at all earlier levels. Guttman's *Scalogram Analysis* allows one to check the success or otherwise of hierarchies of items, by examining the proportion of children who suceed on higher levels, having failed on lower ones. The *CSMS* team reviewed any item groupings which resulted in more than eight per cent of children succeeding on harder items having failed on earlier ones.

'In the hierarchy presented for each test paper, therefore, success on easier levels can generally be assumed to be a prerequisite for success on a harder one'.

The Manual describes the statistical issues rather briefly, but provides references to more detailed discussions. From the tables of relevant coefficients produced, one can be confident that the Tests are reasonable reflections of their designers' intentions.

Data are provided on the facilities of each item, and frequencies of particular errors. The distribution of pupils shown amongst the different levels of understanding on each Test is shown. Data presented on item facilities are worthy of study in their own right. The great differences in facility for children, engendered by changes in the question that, to sophisticated adults, appear to be rather small, are interesting. So too are the frequencies of different responses – especially in cases where specific wrong answers occur ten or more times more commonly than correct responses! Interestingly, questions which require explanation are often poorly answered. Information about the distribution of levels of understanding in larger samples is likely to be of rather limited use to test users, however. Even the larger samples are often rather small; there are obvious problems about their representativeness with respect to one's own class; we do not know the amount of exposure which these samples had to the topic in hand; no error statistics are available to calculate the reliability of perceived differences in proportions of pupils at different levels, and so on. Such criticisms are not very serious, however, because the primary objectives of the Test are to gain insight into the understanding of pupils, and their misconceptions, rather than to examine the overall performance of different groups.

Reliability and **validity** were addressed as follows:
'The usual coefficients of reliability ... were not considered appropriate since in diagnostic tests the items are designed to be of different levels of difficulty and to test different aspects of the concept area. Four tests were used twice with large samples of children, the results being very consistent. Similar consistency was apparent in the results of the longitudinal study which was carried out over three years in the topics of Algebra, Graphs and Ratio. This all suggests that the tests are reliable measures... The measures of scalability [that is, statistics used in the construction of the hierarchies] ... provide further evidence both of reliability and validity.'

For 'many children' (number unspecified) scores on standardized unspecified computation tests were obtained and correlated with their scores on the Number Operations Test; results 'were reasonably high ($\simeq$ 0.65), but several children with high Number Operations scores had low scores for Computation. More traditional tests may therefore under-rate a child's understanding of the four basic number operations'. This information is of little use.

The association between some of the Tests was evaluated when data permitted. Kruskal's *gamma* was used to measure

'the difference between the probability that two individuals chosen at random will have the same ordering on both tests, and the probability that one will score higher on one test and lower on the other.'

No data are provided about sample composition, nor about sample size. It is extremely unlikely that the same children took all the Tests; consequently the comparability of these data is questionable. In general, the data suggest that pupils who attain high levels of understanding on one test do so on others, 'although ... the relationship was by no means exact'.

Using the Tests

Overall guidance on test **administration** is offered, together with detailed instructions which refer to individual Tests. Tests are suitable both for class use, and as the basis for a diagnostic interview with an individual or small group.

'... it is recommended that children are told that the teacher is interested in the way they think about mathematics, so that the best sort of teaching materials to help them individually can be found.'

Tests should be given under examination conditions; pupils may ask questions about the wording of items, and items can be read aloud to pupils whose reading skills are poor. Papers should be collected and assessed in the order in which children are sitting, so that any collaboration can be spotted.

Several Tests present practice questions, which must be worked through before the test proper begins. *Fractions 1* and *Fractions 2* have supplementary tests of computational skill.

Pencils are required; *Ratio and Proportion*, *Reflection and Rotation*, and *Vectors* require rulers marked in centimetres; for *Measurement*, no rulers are necessary; for *Place Value and Decimals* no calculators should be allowed.

Tests are untimed; all working is to be shown on the test paper.

Instructions for **scoring** are clear; scoring keys are provided for each Test which not only provide information about correct answers, but also the most likely wrong answers to each item. Acetate overlays are provided to facilitate scoring of those Tests which require a good deal of construction or drawing by pupils, such as *Rotation and Reflection*. The marking schemes suggest that answers be coded, not simply marked as being right or wrong.

Code 1 is given for correct responses; Code 9 signifies any unidentified errors, and Codes 2 to 8 are used to code specific wrong answers. Of course, not all error codes are applied to all items; not all items include a set of error codes. Not all items are used to assess levels of understanding.

At the side of each item, a box indicates the 'level of under-standing' to which it relates (or is absent). Boxes are ticked if items are answered correctly; subsequently, totals are derived for each level and are transferred to the front of the booklet. Pass or failure at each level depends on answering two-thirds of the available items correctly; each pupil's level of understanding is defined to be the highest level attained. Success at higher levels, associated with failure at lower levels, should be explored further.

A classification into levels of understanding can be made solely on the basis of correct scores. However, the Manual recommends that class performance be analysed by error code on each question for each pupil; it shows how an appropriate class analysis sheet can be prepared. Such sheets should have been pre-printed, and provided with the Tests.

The Manual provides details of the incidence of various error responses. It also describes methods which children used to derive particular answers (on the basis of interviews).

Interpretation of results is a fascinating process! For *Algebra*, a detailed description of common pupil misconceptions is offered; these are related to the levels of understanding in the hierarchy. There is no detailed description of individual items; nor are there any explicit suggestions for remedial teaching.

For *Fractions 1 and 2*, each item is described, together with the demands it makes on the pupil. The levels of understanding in the hierarchy are described. Common misconceptions and 'child-methods' are discussed, item by item. Suggestions for remedial teaching are generally implicit, but occasionally explicit.

For *Graphs*, each item is described, together with common errors and likely underlying misconceptions. Levels of understanding within the hierarchy are described. Teaching suggestions are implicit.

For *Measurement*, item descriptions are provided together with descriptions of common errors and the likely misconceptions which underlie them. The levels of understanding within the hierarchy are described; no teaching suggestions are offered.

Number Operations are treated differently to other topics in the series, and no attempt is made to describe levels of understanding. The Test offers a check that pupils do not have fundamental gaps in their basic knowledge which might dramatically hinder performance on other tests. Answers are coded as being correct; 'basically correct but the wrong way round' (for example, choosing an answer '2 − 8' instead of '8 − 2'); and inverted (for example, choosing '2 + 6'). A classification is offered for addition and subtraction, multiplication and division. Items are not described separately, nor are suggestions made about remedial teaching.

For *Place-Value and Decimals*, the levels of understanding are described in detail, as is the test content. In addition, an analysis of each item is offered, in terms of common pupil misconceptions. No teaching suggestions are offered.

For *Ratio and Proportion*, the levels of understanding are described; so too are common misconceptions. Each item is described individually, in terms of commonly-employed solution methods, and typical errors. No teaching suggestions are offered.

For *Reflection and Rotation*, responses for reflection are categorized as being correct; adequate; containing an overt error (such as reflecting 'horizontally' when the mirror line is slanting); and 'other error'. Problems are categorized into two types, and strategies for solving each are described. For rotation, responses are coded as correct; position of nearest image point correct; slope of image correct; and 'other errors'. In items which involve both reflection and rotation, responses are coded as being completely correct; having a correct final image; and other responses. The detailed scoring scheme for each section focuses entirely on analysis of the responses, and not on underlying causes of error. Levels of understanding are identified, presumably almost entirely on statistical grounds, and are described rather loosely in terms of descriptions of the tasks which can be performed. No teaching suggestions are offered.

For *Vectors* the levels of understanding are described in detail. Questions are described individually in terms of what they assess, and likely pupil errors. No teaching suggestions are offered.

On any test, the simplest analysis is to examine total scores, however 'Simply totalling the marks will provide a "class order", but will give no information on the difficulties of individual children'.

More sensibly, one can examine the level of attainment on a particular topic, and use it as the basis for future teaching.

> '... children need experience with problems of the type that they have *not* been able to answer from the levels they have attained, in order to consolidate their present understanding. The next steps would involve work with ideas of the type found in problems in the next hardest one, or two, levels, depending on what proportion of these questions a child can already successfully answer.'

More detailed guidance to pupils might be offered on the basis of an analysis of particular error codes on any test.

> 'Very often it has been possible to suggest reasons why a particular error occurs... Teachers should be aware of these suggested reasons, since any child who consistently produces a particular type of wrong answer may be in need of specific, directed help in order to change his approach.'

More time-consuming still, but quite consistent with the spirit of the times:

> '... teachers would probably find it extremely revealing to talk to individual children about their strategies... Asking a child to talk about his methods will yield considerable information on the source of his difficulties. One of the major findings of the *CSMS* research ... has been the identification of the "child-methods" employed... These are not teacher-taught, but provide adequate answers for easier questions. Their limitations appear when the complexity of the question is increased.'

(For example, a rule of thumb such as 'multiplication makes bigger' works perfectly when applied to whole numbers, but fails when applied to fractions.)

> 'Teachers should look carefully at the incorrect answers to these problems, since there might be a commonly-occurring wrong answer in the class being tested.'

Rough normative comparisons can be made by comparing individuals, and whole classes, with the larger samples tested in the survey, in terms of their levels of understanding. Comparisons should be treated with some caution, for the reasons set out under *Test development*.

Evaluation

These Tests arose directly from the *CSMS* project, which set out to describe pupils' understanding of mathematics, and their misconceptions, in a number of different topic areas. The *CSMS* project is one of the landmarks in mathematical education, in part because of the evidence it provided about childrens' methods of solution in a wide range of mathematical domains. Children often apply incomplete algorithms perfectly, rather than apply complete algorithms making execution errors. Education is far more likely to succeed if we take account of these incomplete algorithms, misconceptions and the like, and begin teaching from there, rather than by demonstrating perfect performance and asking pupils to copy it. This set of diagnostic Tests is an excellent starting point for the former approach.

Tests are well presented, and interesting. Overall, there is a strong emphasis on assessing pupils' understanding of mathematics rather than on testing their technical skills. The *Teacher's Guide* is informative, and illuminating. Descriptions of items in terms of what they attempt to measure is most welcome; so too are descriptions of patterns of correct responses, and errors, and suggestions about underlying misconceptions. Analysis of levels of understanding is interesting, and generally helpful, and rarely reflects statistical, rather than conceptual, interests. Suggestions about remediation of misconceptions are somewhat lacking, however. It seems sound advice to present pupils with problems that are likely to be accessible to them, but this is hardly the point of diagnosis.

There is a good deal of research work in progress to explore the efficacy of 'diagnostic teaching', where pupils are faced with problems which give answers they can see are obviously wrong, if they bring common misconceptions to bear. It is hoped that their old methods will be willingly swapped for new ones which yield more plausible answers. Hopefully, future editions of the Manual will report on the uses of diagnostic testing and teaching in classrooms, linked to the use of these Tests.

The tests are not completely free of problems: one question refers to an exchange rate of £1 to 1⅗ Australian dollars; another to minced beef at 88.2 pence per kilogram. One *Graphs* question asserts that a plant grew at a constant rate, yet the first three points are not colinear. Occasionally, allowable responses seem strange; for example when pupils are asked for the coordinate of a point reflected in a line, both (14,2) and (2,14) are accepted as correct responses. Details of scoring are not always clear; for example in *Graphs*, Questions 11(d) and 11(f) exist in the margin and in the item facility data, but not on the question sheet. However, the overall presentation and attention to detail is high.

These Tests can be recommended for the purposes of identifying misconceptions in pupil performance; forming the basis for discussion with pupils; offering outline suggestions for teaching (at least as far as the order of presentation of subtopics within major themes is concerned). The *Teacher's Guide* provides many foci for reflecting on the nature of mathematical knowledge, and its acquisition.

GRADED ARITHMETIC – MATHEMATICS TEST

P.E. Vernon and K.M. Miller
First Published 1949; Standardization
date not given; Test Revised 1971;
1976; Manual Revised 1971, 1976
Hodder and Stoughton, UK
Junior 5:03 to 11:08; Senior 11:06
to 18+ (ages not stated)
Group
Timed; 30 mins
Standard Scores in three-month age
bands; Mathematical Ages
Consumable booklets

JUNIOR TEST
Item Distribution

	Number	Measurement	Space	Algebra	Logic	Statistics
Comprehension	12	2	2	–	2	–
Technique	36	1	–	7	–	1
Recall	8	–	1	–	–	–

Presentation						
Words	Numbers	Algebra	Figures	Graphs	Pictures	Oral
38	69	7	3	2	–	–

Response			
Free Format	Forced Choice	Constructed Lines	Explanation
64	6	–	–

Context		
Abstract	Concrete	Total
50	20	70

SENIOR TEST
Item Distribution

	Number	Measurement	Space	Algebra	Logic	Statistics
Comprehension	12	2	7	2	1	1
Technique	21	0	3	14	1	2
Recall	4	–	4	1	–	–

Presentation						
Words	Numbers	Algebra	Figures	Graphs	Pictures	Oral
40	55	22	5	3	–	–

Response			
Free Format	Forced Choice	Constructed Lines	Explanation
64	1	–	–

Context		
Abstract	Concrete	Total
39	26	65

Purposes

'1. Assessing the attainment of individual retarded or problem primary school children by educational psychologists.

2. Grading the mathematical competence of school leavers on entry to technical courses.'

'The Test does not aim to cover specialist mathematics as taught in UK Sixth Forms ... or in colleges. Nevertheless we would suggest that it would be some use as a screening device in first-year university.'

Content

The 1949 edition of this Test consisted of a single test for all ages from 6:00 upwards. The Revised Version consists of a 'Junior' form which presents six to eight items for each school year 6:00 to 12:00. The 'Senior' form is intended for use with pupils from 11:06 upwards. Because of the very great range of age and ability which the tests seek to cover, the items are quite heterogeneous. In the Junior form, 70 items emphasize number operations on single and multiple digits, fractions and decimals, and the use of elementary algebra, while many other topics are raised in one or two items. Items are often presented in words which require an above minimal language competency. The commonest contexts involve money, time and distance. The authors deliberately excluded items based on weights and liquid measures because of the uncertainty about the date of implementation of a full metric system. Thirty-three of these items are shared with the Senior form: here 65 items in all focus more on fractions, geometry, ratio, algebra and often depend on specific knowledge (of logarithms, factorials, set notation and calculus, for example) rather than conceptual knowledge or use of technique. Again items involve the contexts of money, time and distance.

Test development

The Manual points out that the lack of consensus about content and teaching styles in mathematics and arithmetic makes the development of a general purpose test, aimed at a wide range of age and ability, rather difficult. A large collection of items modelled on different texts was given to 3,000 pupils in Canada and England (date unspecified). 'Those items which covered the desired range of ability most evenly and showed consistent rises with age level … were selected in order to make up the two final tests'. Most of the items tried had to be dropped; those that remained were almost all rather traditional in style.

These two sets were then standardized on 7325 children: 2280 English Infant and Junior; 916 Scottish Infant and Junior; 2029 English Secondary, and 2110 Canadian schoolchildren. The English samples were drawn from representative schools in Northamptonshire 'which was considered to be reasonably representative of the country as a whole'. Attempts were made to supply schools of average level for this area and average classes in each school. The Manual acknowledges the difficulty of this task and give no information about how it was carried out.

Norms are provided by age group in three-month age bands in the form of standard scores (described as 'deviation quotients') as well as 'mathematical ages' separately for UK Senior and Junior children (as well as for Canadian schoolchildren). Standard scores are presented in intervals of five points. Sensibly, scores of less than 70 and above 130 are not provided. Norms for pupils aged between 17 and 18 were obtained from pupils in further education, and show considerably higher scores than those for 16–year-olds. Sex differences are not shown, but the Manual reports that below 10 years no significant differences emerged and above 11 years there was a difference in score of six to eight points in favour of boys.

The only measure of **reliability** derives from correlations between scores on odd and even items for pupils, in a number of classes, aged from eight to 16 years. 'After correction coefficients were all 0.90 or over and the average was 0.92.' It is hard to judge the usefulness of this evidence. These data would correspond to an SEM of 4.2. Users are warned that the scores for younger children are less reliable than those for older ones: the score range is smaller, and there are wider differences between pupils and their mathematical experiences.

No evidence is provided about the **validity** of the Test.

Using the Test

Prior experience of test **administration** is required, since too little detailed advice is given for this Test to be used by a relatively inexperienced tester (especially if it is to be given orally). Pencils and erasers are to be used, but rulers must not be available. For the purposes of individual testing, the Manual suggests that the Test should be preceded by a test of reading: if the child's reading age is 8:00 or less, an oral administration is appropriate. Oral administration is also appropriate for younger pupils. Items are presented in order of increasing difficulty. In the Junior form, older children omit a number of the earlier, easier items depending on their age. Advice on appropriate starting points is given, but need not be applied rigidly. 'The aim is to include sufficient easy items so that all pupils can get three or more right at the beginning, without wasting the time of older or brighter children on very easy questions that they can all manage.' There are no practice items in the Test. For class administration all pupils start at the same place: in the Senior form all pupils start at the first question.

The Manual recommends that **scoring** be done twice, preferably by different markers. Scorers are given considerable discretion to mark mathematically equivalent answers as being correct; they are encouraged to be lenient! The commonest kinds of ambiguity are described (including reversals, answers out of sequence, numbers written as words) and may be marked as correct. The scoring key sets out a column of correct answers, a column of incorrect answers, and a column of wrong answers. No separate scoring key is provided. Some of the allowable answers can be challenged: in Question 24, where the correct answer is £10.22, both 1022 and 1.022 are allowed; in Question 33, where the correct answer is £13.48, 1348 is allowed but *not* 1.348.

On the Senior Test, when pupils are asked to provide the value of *pi* to two places of decimals, the answers 3.14, 3.1, 3.2, 3.16, 3.1416 are all allowed. There are several dubious questions in the Test. For example, pupils are presented with a graph and asked to write down its equation. They must infer that it goes through the origin, and that the scales on the 'x' and 'y' axes are the same. 'Wrong' answers are y = kx, y = 2x + k. Scores are totalled on each page and carried forward to the front sheet, where space is provided for the 'Mathematics Age' and the 'Mathematics Quotient'. The derivation of the standard test score from the raw score is relatively straightforward. The Manual suggests that the standard score be expressed to the nearest five points only, but describes how values can be interpolated. An attempt is made to describe the use of the SEM (described as 'the standard error of a deviation quotient') to indicate a confidence interval around any single score. Unfortunately, the user must first obtain the standard score by interpolation; the Manual also refers to the 95 per cent confidence interval as the 5 per cent confidence interval.

Evaluation

This Test attempts to assess the mathematical ability of the whole school age and ability range over 102 items, each with a rather traditional 'text book' flavour. It is necessarily a rather coarsely-grained Test, suitable probably only for screening purposes (such as the rejection of applicants for technical training or for further mathematics courses), or for obtaining an approximate estimate of the mathematical attainment of pupils when no other information is available. Several of the questions and answers are dubious, including two questions on logarithms, and a number, which assess familiarity with mathematical terminology rather than the use of techniques or concepts. Inadequate information is provided about standardization, reliability or validity. The Manual offers much good advice of a general kind, despite some archaic phraseology. It could, however, be better organized, and the description of testing procedures could be made more explicit.

GROUP MATHEMATICS TEST

D. Young
First Published 1970; Standardized 1969, 1977–78; Manual Revised 1980
Hodder and Stoughton, UK
Infants 6:05 – 7:10; first-year Juniors 7:00 – 8.10; second year Juniors and older children 8:00 – 12:10 (6:06 – 12:11)
Group
Part timed, part untimed; (50 mins)
Percentile Ranks in three-month age bands
Consumable sheets

Item Distribution

	Number	Measurement	Space	Algebra	Logic	Statistics
Comprehension	19	2	2	–	6	–
Technique	30	1	2	–	–	–
Recall	–	–	–	–	–	–

Presentation						
Words	Numbers	Algebra	Figures	Graphs	Pictures	Oral
28	51	–	15	–	13	28

Response			
Free Format	Forced Choice	Constructed Lines	Explanation
48	10	–	–

Context		
Abstract	Concrete	Total
34	24	58

Purposes

The Test is one of five tests developed by the author to assess the mathematical ability of children in primary schools. It focuses on upper infants and lower juniors, but can also be used to assess older, less able children. The series of tests 'afford a means of following the progress of children without risking the distortions that can arise from using tests standardized without a common basis'. The Test can be used for the identification of children in need of special education, and for following the progress of an individual child over a period of time.

'Though diagnostic clues can be only incidental in a test primarily designed for general assessment, in a few cases something may be gained' by comparing 'a child's subtest scores (oral with computation or addition with subtraction)'. Such comparisons 'are best made in the light of the school or class averages'. Its use as a diagnostic test is severely limited.

Content

Forms A and B both contain 58 items, comprising two untimed oral sections, and two timed computation sections. The first computation section is made up of 15 addition problems and the second comprises 15 subtraction problems: all these are presented in horizontal form. Both oral sections consist of a mixture of problems, mainly covering the operations of addition, subtraction, multiplication, counting, fractions, ordering, and matching shapes. These operations are applied to a variety of domains (including areas, shapes, and everyday objects like animals and food). More than half of the items assess addition and subtraction skills directly. When multiplication and division items are added to these, more than two-thirds of the Test is seen to be devoted to the direct application of these rules. The choice of other operations and domains is rather patchy: no rationale is provided for the choice of operations or domains of the eight items which do not assess number skills. The computation items are all presented in horizontal form. While this form is appropriate for calculations which involve single digits, it seems inappropriate for the more difficult items like '114 + 178 = '. Half of the Test is administered orally, so that poor readers are not disadvantaged; nevertheless, the wording of some of the questions requires some above-minimum language skill to unravel the mathematical issues.

Test development

No information is provided about **item preparation**. We learn nothing about the author's intentions, nor about his rules for constructing items. Indirect justification for the very narrow computationally-based test can be found in that '... the same large general factor appears in diverse sets of items and indeed in sets of items which could easily be supposed to be testing quite different aspects of mathematics.'

The second **standardization** was based on a sample of 2327 Infants and Juniors, together with 848 older backward children. This sample is rather small for the purposes of constructing standardized scores across a large age range (6:05 to 12:10). No precise information is provided about the date of standardization ('data collected in 1977 and 1978'), or about the selection of samples of children used in the standardization.

The author conducted a study in which a group of 101 children took the *Group Mathematics Test* and other tests from his 'Y' series, at three different ages, one year apart. The median raw scores of these children corresponded to quotients of 101, 100 and 100, and the author concluded 'The five tests therefore afford a means of following the progress of children without risking the distortions that can arise from using tests standardized without a common basis'.

The two test forms were found by the author to be of equal difficulty. 'The differences between the median scores of the sexes are slight, and equal weight was given to both sexes in producing common norms'. One would like to be assured that the author has looked both for significant differences in mean score between the sexes, and for significant differences between the two regression coefficients of age on score for the two sexes, rather than merely comparing median scores. However, for most of the uses to which the Test is put, small differences will probably be unimportant.

Little evidence is provided directly about the **reliability** of the Test; however, it would be most surprising if a test with such a small variety of items had any reliability coefficient below 0.9. Some idea about internal consistency can be gained from a study of 83 children (ages and nature of sample unspecified). The correlation between the oral and computation section was $r = 0.84$. Using the Spearman-Brown correction for test length to assess the reliability of the whole test gives an r value of 0.91. Discussions of **validity**, provide data which suggest strongly that the reliability of the test is high. The standard errors of measurement are presented for samples of children who were tested on both forms of the Test, with a one-week interval between tests. The overall estimate of the standard error of measurement is 2.7 points (raw score).

'Two investigations show satisfactory concurrent and predictive validity for the *GMT*. The correlation between the *GMT* and the

> *Leicester Number Test...* for 145 children was 0.85... The *GMT* scores of 153 children at 7:2 were correlated with their '*Y*' *Mathematics Series* Y1 scores at 8:2 and their Y2 scores at 9:2. The correlations were: *GMT*/y1, 0.87; *GMT*/Y2, 0.86'

It is difficult to understand the author's claim that these data show satisfactory predictive validity for the *Group Mathematics Test*, since no external criterion of mathematical ability is involved. No data are provided about the range of the children's ages, and a wide range could inflate the estimate of the correlation coefficients if raw scores were employed.

> '... the following correlations, calculated from the scores of 83 children, show a considerable overlap between the oral and computational sections despite their apparent individuality. Moreover, there is a similar overlap between the whole test and an oral verbal intelligence test having no mathematical content': (a) oral section with computation section 0.84; (b) oral section with *Non-Readers Intelligence Test (NRIT)*, 0.79; (c) computation section with *NRIT*, 0.80; (d) Total with *NRIT*, 0.83.

Again, there are difficulties in interpreting these data, and other correlational data offered, because the distributions of the children's ages and of the scores on all the tests are not given. A wide age range can lead to an overestimation of correlation coefficients.

Using the Test

The Test is **administered** in two halves, preferably before and after break. In the oral section, the administrator reads each question aloud and allows seven seconds for the children to write their answers. The computational section is timed for eight minutes.

Less able children can take the Test as four sub-tests; more able children can take the whole Test in one sitting. By giving adjacent rows of pupils different forms of the Test, the risk of copying can be minimized. The Test can be given by one teacher to a full class. Children need a pencil each. The administrator needs a watch with a second hand.

The administrator's script, provided in the Manual, is satisfactory. The importance of ensuring that children understand the items is emphasized. The language used in some of the orally-administered questions could be simplified. It is the author's intention, however, to 'recognize and reinforce ... the place of language in mathematics'.

The **scoring** scheme is straightforward, and is adequately described in the Manual. The scorer's discretion is clearly specified; for example, reversal of figures is allowed, but transposition of digits is not. Right and wrong answers can be marked as such on the answer sheet, and columns totalled easily. Summaries of the four 'subtests' are written on the front of the answer sheet and are added to give the child's total score, which is converted to a standard score via a table. The answer sheet could be improved by providing a space for insertion of the child's age, and for the standard score, alongside the raw score, at the top of the sheet.

Tables of 'Mathematics Quotients', which are standard scores with a mean of 100 and a standard deviation of 15 are provided. The quotients are provided for different test scores, in one-month age bands. Separate tables are provided for infants (6:05 to 7:10); Juniors (7:00 to 8:10); and older pupils (8:00 to 12:10) in three-month age bands. A table relating test score to 'mathematics ages' is provided as 'an alternative scale for very backward children whose quotients may be difficult to interpret in practical terms'.

The **interpretation** of scores is quite direct. Normative comparisons are made with data provided in the Manual or between pupils. Sensibly, given the purposes of the Test and the size of the standardization sample, standardized scores outside the range 70 to 130 are simply recorded as '< 70' or '> 130'.

The Manual points out that the content of the Test is far too limited for the higher scores of first-year Juniors to have much meaning, and that the use of 'mathematical ages' is provided as a very rough rule of thumb when testing very backward children.

Evaluation

The Test purports to measure the mathematical ability of Infants and first-year Juniors, and is one of a series of tests designed to assess children aged 6:06 to 11:10. It can also be used for older, less able children. The format of some of the items presents the children with difficulties that are irrelevant to the mathematical operations to be performed.

The range of items chosen is very narrow, focusing almost exclusively on the four basic operations. In my view, there is a considerable danger in the view that mathematical attainment in the first few years of primary school can be assessed by examining technique on the basic operations alone. Pupils should *not* be introduced to mathematics as if it were a collection of problems with no familiar context, to be solved by the application of hard algorithms. The Test is *not* a mathematics test. It should be relabelled 'Computation Skills', or something similar.

The Manual is deficient in a number of respects. Most important, the user is presented with inadequate data that do not make possible an assessment of reliability and validity. No data are provided on the nature of the standardization sample. Less important, the style is turgid, and the contents need to be rearranged to make them more readily accessible to the user.

The Test is of some use in that it can be used to point out children who are performing below par on basic mathematical operations. The fact that it is one of a series of tests allows the progress of an individual child to be followed over a period of time. However, the philosophy implicit in the choice of items concerning the nature of mathematics in primary schools is sufficiently pernicious to outweigh the Test's usefulness for other purposes.

LEICESTER NUMBER TEST

W.E.C. Gillham and K.A. Hesse
First Published 1970; Standardized
1968 (first-year Juniors), 1972
(second-year Juniors); Manual
Revised 1973
Hodder and Stoughton, UK
7:01–9:00 (7:01–9:00)
Group, Oral
Untimed; (50 mins)
Standard Scores in one-year age
bands; Percentiles
Consumable booklets

Item Distribution

	Number	Measurement	Space	Algebra	Logic	Statistics
Comprehension	20	–	2	–	10	–
Technique	51	–	–	–	–	–
Recall	1	–	–	–	–	–

Presentation						
Words	Numbers	Algebra	Figures	Graphs	Pictures	Oral
49	66	–	23	–	1	48

Response			
Free Format	Forced Choice	Constructed Lines	Explanation
53	10	16	–

Context		
Abstract	Concrete	Total
47	27	74

Purposes

The Test was 'designed for use with children entering the junior department of a primary school... to assess a child's under-standing of basic concepts of the number system as well as his grasp of the "four rules" of conventional calculation. It is particularly constructed to discriminate amongst the least able 25 per cent of the age-groups...'

'It is certainly not claimed that this is a test of the "new mathematics"... The Test is designed:

a) to indicate areas of weakness in individual children;

b) to provide a basis for grouping for teaching;
c) to detect gross educational failure, as part of a comprehensive attainment assessment programme;
d) to make possible a continuous appraisal of attainment in number through the Junior school;
e) to give some guidance as to the content and emphasis of an essential part of primary school mathematics.'

Content

Items focus on counting, arithmetic operations on single and multiple digits, and ordering, with a few items devoted to knowledge about fractions, and extending patterns. Items most commonly involve reading and writing numbers, or counting up familiar shapes. Items are clearly printed. The Test is presented orally, and so reading difficulties are avoided. The non-scoring practice items are very easy; the first 20 test items are easy, both to encourage children unfamiliar with the test format, and to discriminate amongst lower attainers.

Test development

The authors set out to test most of those aspects of number which the Schools Council document *Mathematics in Primary Schools: Curriculum Bulletin No.1* describes as the 'mathematical concepts which it is possible for most children to learn by the age of seven years'. The topics of measurement, money, shape and size were deliberately excluded. They attempted to cover: counting, number equivalence, relative size, grouping, simple fractions, and use of the basic operations. The authors refer to two earlier versions of the Test, but give no more details about test development.

The Test was **standardized** in the City of Leicester in October, 1968; a week later the Test was readministered so that test-retest reliability could be assessed. Standard scores are presented, based on 557 non-immigrant children in six schools (284 boys, 273 girls), aged 7:01 to 8:01. The authors set out to obtain a stratified sample, which they believed to be representative of Leicester school children. Users are warned that they will be comparing scores with children from Leicester but are reassured that this sample is unlikely to be significantly different from a nationally based sample of other urban areas. A second, and similar, standardizing sample consisted of 469 non-immigrant pupils (236 girls, and 233 boys) aged 8:00 to 9:00 who were tested in September 1972 as part of the standardization of the *Nottingham Number Test*. Users are referred to the *Nottingham Number Test* Manual for details.

The raw score distribution is negatively skewed, because of the authors' intentions to discriminate amongst low-attaining pupils. Standard scores are presented (called 'quotients') for each year band (7:01 to 8:01; 8:00 to 9:00), together with percentile scores. No age-allowance is made; no information is presented about sex differences.

Test-retest **reliability**, based on 512 children from the original Leicester standardization group was found to be 0.92, which corresponds to an SEM of 4.2 points. For the older Nottingham children it was 0.91, which corresponds to an SEM of five points. The authors chose not to offer measures of internal consistency. The Manual asserts that, since the Test directly assesses what we seek to measure, and given that its reliability is acceptably high, judgements based on *surface validity* are appropriate. *Concurrent validity* was assessed via the administration of the *NFER Picture Test 1* and *NFER Mechanical Arithmetic Test 2A* to the standardizing sample. Correlations with the *Leicester Number Test* were 0.59 and 0.64 respectively. No unambiguous interpretation can be made from these data. Some further data are presented concerning the *concurrent validity* of the Test based on teacher estimates of the number ability of 95 children. Teachers had known the pupils for four weeks when these ratings were made; pupils were split into seven groups and the correlation between average ratings and scores on the *Leicester Number Test* was found to be 0.69. Again, it is difficult to interpret these data unequivocally.

Using the Test

The Test is **administered** orally, and is untimed. It should be used by a teacher experienced in test administration (the Manual also recommends a trial run with another group). A stopwatch and spare pencils should be available. The script in the Manual offers sound advice on classroom organization for test administration; details for each question, which are read aloud singly, are clear. The administrator must judge when all the children have finished each question.

The instructions for **scoring** are unambiguous and sensible, for example, on the way reversed figures are to be treated. However, no separate scoring key is provided so the marker must continually cross-check between the answer sheet and the Manual. No spaces are allocated for marks on the sheets, and no provision is made for internal checks of marker accuracy.

A raw score is calculated for each child, which is then converted to a standard score and a percentile. These are both reported as numbers, rather than as score bands. The interpretation of SEM is described in the Manual, and the SEM should have been incorporated into each pupil's score. Interpretation of results is direct and can form the basis for purposes a), c) and possibly b), described above; but not for purposes d) and e) in my view, for reasons set out below.

Evaluation

The Test aims to assess a range of skills focused on the topic of number. Authors begin with clear ideas about those (limited) aspects of number work they wish to focus on, and with evidence about likely pupil attainment at the age of seven. It is a pity that this good beginning is not followed through. The range of problem contexts is rather narrow (since the authors avoid the topics of measurement, money, shape and size) as is the range of number topics. Users are left to work out for themselves how topics in number relate to test items. It would have been useful to users for conceptual and diagnostic purposes to have a clear statement relating scores on different questions to the number of topics covered; a blanket score on a 'Number Test' offers little in the way of suggestions about how things might be improved for pupils (and teachers).

MATHEMATICS 8 TO 12

Test Development Unit of the National Foundation for Educational Research, with Alan Brighouse, David Godber and Peter Patilla
First Published: *8*, 1984; *9–12*, 1983; Manual, 1984; Standardized: *8*, 1984; *9–12*, 1983
NFER-NELSON, UK
Mathematics 8
  Junior School: first year   7:06–8:11 (7:09–8:09)
  First School: final year   7:06–8:11 (7:09–8:09)
Mathematics 9
  Junior School: second year   8:06–9:11 (8:09–9:09)
  Middle School: first year   8:06–9:11 (8:09–9:09)
Mathematics 10
  Junior School: third year   9:06–10:11 (9:09–10:09)
  Middle School: second year   9:06–10:11 (9:09–10:09)
Mathematics 11
  Junior School: fourth year   10:06–11:11 (10:09–11:09)
  Middle School: third year   10:06–11:11 (10:09–11:09)
Mathematics 12
  Secondary School: first year   11:06–12:11 (11:09–12:09)
  Middle School: fourth year   11:06–12:11 (11:09–12:09)
Group; *Mathematics 8* has an oral component
Untimed (45 mins)
Standard Scores in one-month age bands; Percentiles; some diagnostic use
Consumable booklets

MATHEMATICS 8

Item Distribution

	Number	Measurement	Space	Algebra	Logic	Statistics
Comprehension	12	6	2	–	1	–
Technique	12	3	1	–	–	–
Recall	3	1	1	–	–	–

Presentation						
Words	Numbers	Algebra	Figures	Graphs	Pictures	Oral
27	33	–	11	1	4	18

Response			
Free Format	Forced Choice	Constructed Lines	Explanation
27	8	1	–

Context		
Abstract	Concrete	Total
17	19	36

MATHEMATICS 9
Item Distribution

	Number	Measurement	Space	Algebra	Logic	Statistics
Comprehension	11	4	4	–	1	–
Technique	19	6	2	–	–	–
Recall	2	2	4	–	–	–

Presentation						
Words	Numbers	Algebra	Figures	Graphs	Pictures	Oral
37	45	–	16	2	–	–

Response			
Free Format	Forced Choice	Constructed Lines	Explanation
40	10	–	–

Context		
Abstract	Concrete	Total
19	31	50

MATHEMATICS 10
Item Distribution

	Number	Measurement	Space	Algebra	Logic	Statistics
Comprehension	11	8	9	1	2	–
Technique	14	4	3	–	–	–
Recall	3	1	2	–	–	–

Presentation						
Words	Numbers	Algebra	Figures	Graphs	Pictures	Oral
40	43	1	18	4	–	–

Response			
Free Format	Forced Choice	Constructed Lines	Explanation
39	7	4	–

Context		
Abstract	Concrete	Total
17	33	50

MATHEMATICS 11
Item Distribution

	Number	Measurement	Space	Algebra	Logic	Statistics
Comprehension	10	7	5	–	1	–
Technique	17	5	2	–	–	–
Recall	2	1	5	–	–	–

Presentation

Words	Numbers	Algebra	Figures	Graphs	Pictures	Oral
44	45	–	13	4	–	–

Response

Free Format	Forced Choice	Constructed Lines	Explanation
39	9	2	–

Context

Abstract	Concrete	Total
15	35	50

MATHEMATICS 12
Item Distribution

	Number	Measurement	Space	Algebra	Logic	Statistics
Comprehension	10	9	4	1	3	–
Technique	17	4	1	–	–	–
Recall	2	1	1	–	–	–

Presentation

Words	Numbers	Algebra	Figures	Graphs	Pictures	Oral
44	46	1	12	7	1	–

Response

Free Format	Forced Choice	Constructed Lines	Explanation
41	7	2	–

Context

Abstract	Concrete	Total
20	30	50

Purposes

'... thought was given both to curriculum content ... and to broad teaching objectives of primary and early secondary school mathematics. Within the limits of a written test of mathematics attainment, the aim was to include ... questions which sampled across a range of topics ... but which at the same time required demonstrations of the ability to operate at different levels involving varying concepts and skills.'

'... designed primarily to provide an assessment of overall mathematics attainment at the end of the school year.'

'The language of the questions has been simplified as far as possible, to ensure that it is mathematical skill rather than reading ability which is being tested.'

'... the suitability of any individual test within *Mathematics 8–12* should be judged from its content and from a knowledge of the group or individual to be tested.'

While 'each test should primarily be considered as a whole ...' some suggestions are made about how class or group responses to individual questions can be explored.

Mathematics 8–12 is designed for use towards the end of the academic year when pupils reach the age in the Test title; it is intended to provide summative assessment of attainment of work usually encountered in that school year. In addition, the Test can provide information about strengths and weaknesses of pupils (and classes) in particular areas, or on particular groups of tasks, and thus has some diagnostic function.

Content

Mathematics 8–12 comprises five tests, each aimed at a school year, and a single *Teachers' Guide* which is used with every test. Class record sheets are available. The content of the tests is described as follows:

Mathematics 8

NUMBER
Place-value, formal and informal computation in the four number operations involving hundreds, tens and units, series, computation, and problems involving money.

MEASUREMENT
Simple area estimation and measuring of length, height, weight and capacity, telling time and calendar work.

SHAPE
Names of solid shapes, tessellations, rotation.

PICTORIAL REPRESENTATION
Block graph (scale of 1:1).

Mathematics 9

NUMBER
Place-value, computation in the four number operations involving hundreds, tens and units, simple fractions, computation, and problems involving money.

MEASUREMENT
Simple area, telling the time, calendar work, length, capacity, weight, right angle.

SHAPE
Names of plane and solid shapes.

PICTORIAL REPRESENTATION
Block graph (Scale of 1:1).

Mathematics 10

NUMBER
Place-value, formal computation in the four number operations involving thousands, hundreds, tens and units, average, fractions of quantities, decimals to one place, money.

MEASUREMENT
Angles, points of a compass, weight, volume, time in minutes and seconds, length, capacity.

SHAPE
Reflection, parts of a circle, simple co-ordinates; names of plane and solid shapes.

PICTORIAL REPRESENTATION
Reading a scale, interpretation of a block graph.

Mathematics 11

NUMBER
Place-value, formal computation in the four number operations involving thousands, hundreds, tens and units, decimals to three places, percentage, average, equivalence of coins, general money problems, fractions.

MEASUREMENT
Weight, length, area, volume, time, scale, angles.

SHAPE
Co-ordinates, plane and solid shapes.

PICTORIAL REPRESENTATION
Mapping, line graph, pie chart.

Mathematics 12

NUMBER
Structure of a number, place-value, computation in the four number operations involving thousands, hundreds, tens and units, relationships, percentages, algebraic notation, decimals to three places, money, fractions, square roots and square numbers, Venn diagram, time (24–hour clock).

MEASUREMENT
Volume, capacity, angles, weight, temperature, length, area.

SHAPE
Nets, plane and solid shapes, co-ordinates.

PICTORIAL REPRESENTATION
Curved line graph, pictorial graph, pie chart.

As well as classifying items in terms of content, each is classified in terms of four skill areas, described as *factual recall* (requiring 'basic knowledge' but no calculation); *computation* (where operations are given explicitly, in order to test computational skill); *application* (where questions test the ability to deploy mathematical skills in everyday situations; operations are rarely stated explicitly, and some language skills are usually required); and *understanding* (which involve the interpretation of mathematical language and the understanding of the basic concepts involved before they can be answered correctly).

The Manual presents a table of problem types, arranged to illustrate the skills/content links.

Test development

Tests were constructed largely from the *NFER Mathematics Item Bank*, which is a collection of items written over a five-year period 'to include the common elements of many mathematics schemes and many LEAs' guidelines'. All the questions in the bank have to be tried out at least once on groups of 300 or more children. Questions which proved to be too easy, or which failed to discriminate between children, were excluded. Questions were assembled in accordance with the blueprint in the Manual for each year group. Several items have appeared earlier in Schools Council publications.

'questions [are] selected to assess across as broad a curriculum as possible. ... each question has been carefully considered for its demand on a child's knowledge, skills and understanding, and a specially devised coding scheme has been incorporated into the design of the test booklets to enable teachers to investigate the performances of their groups'.

Tests early in the series focus more on understanding and computation. Later tests present fewer items on computation, and more items on application. Items do *not* increase in difficulty throughout any test, in order to maintain pupils' motivation.

Mathematics 8 was developed in 1983 and standardized in the summer of 1984. *Mathematics 9, 10, 11* and *12* were compiled during 1981–82 and 'were standardized in the summer of 1983 on representative samples of the United Kingdom's population of school children'.

Each Test was **standardized** separately:

'In each case a random sample of schools was drawn from the national register, and within each school, all the pupils in the appropriate age range were tested. The samples were stratified by a series of variables, giving a more accurate representation of the country as a whole. These variables were geographical region ... school type, size of the year-group within the school, and finally a metropolitan versus non-metropolitan categorization.'

In all, 437 schools took part, involving a total of 16,142 pupils. The Manual itemizes the number of schools, pupils, mean raw score and standardization date for each Test.

Reliability is described both in terms of test-retest reliability, and in terms of internal consistency. KR–20 is quoted for each test, alongside the corresponding SEM; values range from 0.93 to 0.95, corresponding to SEM of 4.0 to 3.3. Unaccountably, no information is provided about the samples on which these data are based – not even sample size.

Validity is described. The Tests are justified in terms of content validity and the blueprint of mathematical behaviours which underlies the choice of items. A study of construct validity was also conducted. In 22 of the schools which took part in the 1983 test standardization exercise, teachers were asked to rank pupils in order of their overall 'mathematical progress', taking no account of their relative ages. Rankings were correlated with standard scores via Spearman's *rho*. Values ranged from 0.74 to 0.95: median for *Mathematics 9* was 0.86 (nine schools); similar values were found for other tests. These '... indicate that the tests are providing scores which are broadly in the same order as the teachers' understanding of the progress of their pupils'. Comparable results are expected for *Mathematics 8*. One school had administered subtests M1 (Concepts) and M2 (Problem Solving) of the *Richmond Tests of Basic Skills* as well as *Mathematics 11*. Correlations between standard scores were 0.80 with M1, and 0.85 with M2 and *Mathematics 11* for this tiny (38 pupils) accidental sample. 'This result adds to the validity of *Mathematics 8* to *Mathematics 12* since it indicates that the measures are broadly in line with those obtained from other standardized mathematics tests.'

These two studies of concurrent validity are referred to rather strangely as 'evidence of criterion-related validity'. It is odd that the authors bother to describe a study based on only 38 pupils: if this sort of approach to concurrent validity is worth doing, it should be done more systematically, and on larger samples.

Using the Test

Tests should be **administered** during the Summer Term, if test norms are to be used. Testing should take place in the pupils' usual teaching room; if this is not possible, pupils should be tested in a room familiar to them.

Pupils require a pencil and an eraser; a ruler may be useful but is not essential. The purpose of the Test should be explained to pupils as, for example, 'to help find out what you can do and where you need more help'. A detailed script is provided for *Mathematics 8*. Details of test administration are exemplary.

Tests are untimed; they are designed to be given in a double lesson of 60 to 80 minutes, and the majority of children are expected to finish within 45 to 50 minutes. 'Pupils who are likely to take more than one hour can probably be identified beforehand, and it may be necessary to make special arrangements for these'.

Mathematics 8 consists of two distinct halves which can be given separately. For younger children, teachers should fill in the personal details on the front of each test booklet before handing them out.

Instructions for **scoring** are clear; the Manual provides a marking key, sectioned so as to correspond with each page in each test booklet (although not perfectly aligned with the booklet answers). Page totals are summed and transferred to the front of the test booklet; no checks are provided against scorer errors. Raw scores are converted to standard scores and percentiles, then transferred to a score line, which contains not only descriptions such as 'moderately low score' but also provides the number of points of standard score to be added and subtracted to provide a 90 per cent confidence interval.

The Manual warns against the use of test norms if children are not tested in the Summer Term. It also warns against the administration of a test other than the one recommended for the age group concerned.

'The **interpretation** of results falls naturally into two parts: a statistical appraisal of the scores derived from the test, and a more qualitative assessment of how an individual child's performance on the test can assist in understanding his or her progress with a view to providing the most appropriate learning experiences in the future'.

The rationale underlying the use of standard scores is described, along with their relationship to percentiles. The Manual emphasizes that scores obtained are 'only *estimates* of a child's standing relative to a larger peer group'. Users are warned against over interpretation of percentiles because of their sensitivity to small changes in raw scores, and the difficulty of assessing errors of measurement.

Reliability, SEM, and confidence intervals are explained clearly; 90 per cent confidence intervals are suggested. Because confidence intervals are only distributed symmetrically close to the mean, the front of each booklet provides a number line on which a pupil's score is recorded, together with the number of points of standard score which are to be added and subtracted in order to provide a 90 per cent confidence interval. So for a standard score of 80 on *Mathematics 12*, one adds seven and subtracts five, and for a standard score of 135 one adds five and subtracts eight. The incorporation of SEM into the report of scores is clearly a good thing; the provision of easy methods for calculation is to be applauded.

A group record sheet has been provided to facilitate an examination of whole class performance: '... this can have important implications both for re-teaching the children who have been tested and for the curriculum in subsequent years'. The sheet summarizes performance on each item for each pupil; it also classifies each item in terms of the skills it demands, and shows the percentage of pupils in the standardizing sample who got the question correct. When group performance is 10 or more percentage points lower than the standardizing sample, the causes need to be explored; the Manual warns against over-interpreting results from small groups. (Similarly, performance on single items might offer pointers, but should not be taken to be reliable evidence about lack of attainment).

The Manual recommends that items on which performance is unexpectedly low should be grouped together under their skill headings to try and spot areas in need of further class work. Similar clues can be provided by omitted items.

'Examining the kinds of questions which have unexpectedly low proportions correct, both in terms of the skill areas and the mathematics topic involved, may indicate that particular remedial action is desirable.'

Some suggestions are offered 'as to how weaknesses in the four skill areas ... may be tackled...' Suggestions are brief and bland: *understanding* can be developed 'using appropriate apparatus and language' and by 'experience in as many ways as possible'; *computation* skills can be improved by practising skills in a considered, structured manner, increasing difficulty steadily ('the cause of the error must ... be diagnosed and ... remedied by appropriate action'); *application* skills need practice, and depend on earlier skills of understanding and computation; *factual recall* requires extra practice and revision where errors are due to carelessness or memory lapses, and further teaching if they are due to a lack of understanding or have not yet been introduced.

Evaluation

Mathematics 8–12 sets out to provide a summative evaluation of mathematical attainment in each of five school years, together with some diagnostic help for individual pupils, and for whole classes. An effort has been made to describe the test designers' intentions, and the blueprint for test construction is provided.

Users can therefore judge readily the suitability of the Test for their needs. Items are well presented, and reasonably interesting, although two questions cause mild concern about the balance between accuracy and realism: one of these, which involves dividing up cakes, requires answers correct to one gram; the other features a population growth curve that smoothly ignores the predations of two world wars. Pupils are unlikely to be bothered, however.

Tests were standardized with great care. Issues of validity are left to the judgement of users. Details of administration are good; scoring is easy, and important issues concerning the use of norms, SEM and the like, are explained clearly and well. The adoption of a score band to record pupil performance, and the provision of an easy method to calculate these bands for different standard scores, is most welcome.

Users are encouraged to examine group performance on individual items, relating it to success rate of the standardizing sample. Individual items will be rather unreliable measures of performance, but the exercise of thinking about the *skills* assessed by particular items, and the ways that these skills can be developed in class, is useful. The grouping of items into recall, computation, application and understanding can also be a help to teachers' reflection on their personal teaching emphases. The recommendations for remediation of poor performance are rather bland; references to other sources, such as publications of the Association of Teachers of Mathematics and the Mathematical Association publications might be helpful.

Overall, this series of Tests is to be recommended. The principles of test construction are clearly set out; it has been carefully standardized; technical issues are explained clearly; the Manual is well-written, and testing and scoring are straightforward; sensible advice is offered about how test results can be interpreted and used.

MATHEMATICS ATTAINMENT TEST A

National Foundation for Educational Research
First Published 1970; Standardized 1969–71; Test Revision 1978; Manual Revision 1970
NFER-NELSON, UK
7:00–8:06 (6:09–8:02)
Group, Oral
Untimed; (45 mins)
Standard Scores in one-month age bands
Consumable booklets

Item Distribution

	Number	Measurement	Space	Algebra	Logic	Statistics
Comprehension	20	3	9	–	3	–
Technique	8	3	2	–	–	–
Recall	1	1	1	–	–	–

Presentation						
Words	Numbers	Algebra	Figures	Graphs	Pictures	Oral
38	35	–	17	3	6	42

Response			
Free Format	Forced Choice	Constructed Lines	Explanation
25	12	5	–

Context		
Abstract	Concrete	Total
16	26	42

The *Mathematics Attainment Test* series has been replaced by the *Basic Mathematics Test* series. The review of *Mathematics Attainment Test A* reveals the nature of the changes made.

Purposes

'… to provide a measure of mathematics attainment of first-year junior school children.'

'… to test the child's grasp of a wide range of mathematical ideas …'

Content

Forty-two items cover the use of a number of operations, including adding, subtracting, multiplying, dividing, counting, ordering, classifying and equating. These operations are applied to the topics of fractional parts, area, money, bar charts, size, volume, weight, place value, shape, length, and telling the time.

Test Development

No data are presented about how the items were developed, nor is there any information about any pilot studies which may have been conducted.

The Test was **standardized** on all the first-year children in primary schools in five selected areas (unspecified) during the school years 1969–70 and 1970–71. The scores were collected from 3,515 boys and 3,249 girls, whose mean age was 7:10. No information is provided about the nature of these 'selected areas', and so the normative data can be used only as a rough guide to the relative performance of any individual or group under consideration.

The only reported measure of **reliability** is KR–20 calculated from a sample of 259 scripts obtained from one of the representative standardization samples. A value of 0.94 corresponds to a standard error of measurement of 3.66. The Manual explains in a straightforward manner how this value is to be interpreted and used when comparing individuals.

No **validity** studies are reported. Inspection of the test items provides clues about the content validity of the test items. Since the Test is a measure of mathematical attainment, items have been chosen which reflect topics commonly dealt with in first-year junior mathematics. Their design seems to follow no systematic pattern; some operations seem over-represented, and tied to specific topics (three questions on fractions all use shaded areas); others seem to be under-represented.

Using the Test

The Test is **administered** orally to overcome the problems which poor readers face when presented with written mathematics problems. The Test requires pupils to understand spoken English and to possess elementary writing skills. 'The proper administration of an oral test requires particular skill and it is recommended that this test should be given by an experienced teacher.' Each child needs a response booklet, and a pencil. The Test takes 30 to 60 minutes to administer, depending on the speed of the children's work. It is recommended that the Test should not be given to a group of more than 45 children. Questions are read aloud by the test administrators, one item at a time. The administrator has to judge when all the children have finished each question, before proceeding to the next.

The script for administering the Test is perfectly clear. One improvement might be made. Pupils are asked to write their date of birth on the front of the response booklet: this seems a difficult thing for a child aged 7:00 to do and it would probably be better if these data were taken from the class register by the teacher.

The instructions for **scoring** are clear for the most part. However, although the marker is instructed to allow mis-spelled items to be counted as correct, no guidance is given on numbers which are written in mirror form, or with digits reversed (61 to 16, for example). The scoring sheet provides some check against errors in scoring.

Two items require children to draw hands on a clock face provided, to represent 'a quarter to one', and '25 past nine'. In the sample answers, regions of acceptability for the position of the hands are provided. However, in both cases, the centre of the regions point directly at the relevant number on the clock face. Thus for '25 past nine', the answer is accepted if the minute hand is in the region 23 to 27, and the hour hand in the region 43 to 47. So an answer where the hour hand points at 48, and the minute hand at 25 is 'wrong', but if the hour hand points at 43 and the minute hand at 27, it is 'right'.

A raw score is calculated for each child. The Manual provides a conversion table which allows the user to determine the *standard score* for each child, using the raw score and the child's age. The Manual provides a guide to the **interpretation** of these standard scores in terms of the percentage of children who attained less than a given standard score.

'... in the standardization sample the superiority of boys over girls amounted to 1.3 points of standardized score with a standard error of 0.4 points. The difference between the sexes is significant at the one per cent level, therefore it is recommended that in all assessments with this test the two sexes be considered independently of each other, unless it has been shown that the sex difference is not present in the sample tested.'!

Separate sex norms, however, are not presented.

Each child is given a raw score and a standard score purporting to reflect mathematical attainment. These scores allow the user to relate children to classroom peers, and both the child and a class to a large (unspecified) sample of schoolchildren from the same age range. However, since the Test has no diagnostic function, the scores can be used only as a source of either congratulation or exhortation to try harder to learn (and teach). No prescriptions for improving performance can be made, unless teachers themselves analyse the Test in terms of the difficulty of the items for the class, and in terms of the possible content validity of the most difficult items.

Evaluation

Items are well presented, and cover a wide range of operations and contexts. The Manual is well written and easy to use. Details of test administration are clear, but advice on scoring could be more explicit about the treatment of reversed digits. Too little information is provided about the standardization sample, and the presence of a sex difference in scores also gives cause for concern. A score band would be preferable to a single score. *Basic Mathematics Test A* was developed from this Test and, as the former offers significant advantages, it should be used in preference to *Mathematics Attainment Test A*.

MATHEMATICS ATTAINMENT TEST B

National Foundation for Educational Research
First Published 1970; Standardized 1965, 1977; Test Revised 1970; Manual Revised 1978
NFER-NELSON, UK
8:00–10:06 (8:00–10:08)
Group
Untimed; (45 mins)
Standard Scores in one-month age bands; separately for second– and third-year Juniors
Consumable booklets

Item Distribution

	Number	Measurement	Space	Algebra	Logic	Statistics
Comprehension	23	3	8	–	6	–
Technique	3	3	2	1	2	–
Recall	4	–	1	–	–	–

Presentation						
Words	Numbers	Algebra	Figures	Graphs	Pictures	Oral
35	40	1	18	2	4	42

Response			
Free Format	Forced Choice	Constructed Lines	Explanation
25	12	5	–

Context		
Abstract	Concrete	Total
16	26	42

The *Mathematics Attainment Test* series has been replaced by the *Basic Mathematics Test* series. The detailed review of *Mathematics Attainment Test A* can be compared with the review of *Basic Mathematics Test A* in order to see the nature of the changes made. Only a brief review will be presented here.

Purposes

'to test the mathematical experience and understanding of second-year junior school children.'

Content

Forty-two items focus on single and multiple digit operations, fractions, estimation and approximation, and counting. They are presented most commonly in the form of numbers, geometric figures, shapes or familiar figures, and pupils respond by writing or circling numbers, drawing lines, or shading. The Test is presented orally.

Test Development

Items were constructed by a panel of Worcestershire teachers. A small-scale study demonstrated the need for oral administration of the Test. The Test was **restandardized** on a sample of 7,923 children in second– and third– year junior classes, 'selected according to a stratified random sample technique designed to make it representative of the population in England and Wales'. No significant differences in scores were found between girls and boys, so separate norms are not presented.

Reliability was assessed separately for the second– and third-years by calculating KR–20. Reliabilities were found to be 0.93 and 0.92 respectively, corresponding to SEMs of 4.05 and 4.14. The Manual explains the use of the SEM to reflect the accuracy of any assessment made, and recommends this practice.

No evidence is offered concerning **validity**.

Using the Test

The Test should be **administered** by an experienced teacher; pencils are required, rulers and erasers should not be available. Instructions for administration are clear and sensible.

Marking is straightforward; the scoring key almost aligns with the test booklet; built-in checks help avoid marker errors. Calculation of standard scores is easy; users must already know how to **interpret** results in this form.

Evaluation

The Test offers clearly-presented items on a variety of topics, in a range of contexts. Items are rather too easy if the user wishes to discriminate amongst older, more able children. The Manual is well written and sensibly set out; details of test administration and scoring are quite adequate, although no attention is paid to score interpretation. This Test has been replaced by others in the *Basic Mathematics Test* series. There, tests offer some diagnostic help as well as ordering pupils with respect to each other and a notional national sample.

MATHEMATICS ATTAINMENT TEST C1

Teacher members of the Surrey Educational Research Association First Published 1970; Restandardized 1977; Test Revised 1969; Manual Revised 1970 NFER-NELSON, UK 9:00–12:00 (9:07–11:07) Group Untimed; (50 mins) Standard Scores in one-month age bands; separately for third– and fourth–year Juniors Consumable booklets

Item Distribution

	Number	Measurement	Space	Algebra	Logic	Statistics
Comprehension	27	7	2	–	4	–
Technique	7	5	4	2	3	–
Recall	2	–	–	–	–	–

Presentation						
Words	Numbers	Algebra	Figures	Graphs	Pictures	Oral
50	48	3	12	11	–	–

Response			
Free Format	Forced Choice	Constructed Lines	Explanation
31	19	–	–

Context		
Abstract	Concrete	Total
13	37	50

The *Mathematics Attainment Test* series has been replaced by the *Basic Mathematics Test* series. The detailed review of *Mathematics Attainment Test A* can be compared with the review of *Basic Mathematics Test A* in order to see the nature of the changes made. Only a brief review will be presented here.

Purposes

'It was designed to measure the child's knowledge and understanding of mathematics rather than his mechanical skill. Computation has therefore been kept to a minimum.'

Content

Fifty items are spread across a range of topics, including multiple digit operations, fractions, reading and interpreting information, simple geometry, base, series and number patterns and choice of operation.

Test Development

The Test was constructed by 'a group of primary mathematics teachers working as members of the Surrey Educational Research Association'. The Test was **restandardized** on a sample of 7,250 third– and fourth-year Junior children, 'selected according to a stratified random technique designed to make it representative of the population in England and Wales'. No significant differences in scores were found between girls and boys, so separate norms are not presented.

Reliability was assessed separately for the third– and fourth-years by calculating KR–20. Reliabilities were found to be 0.95 and 0.96, corresponding to SEMs of 3.45 and 3.28 respectively. The Manual explains the use of the SEM to reflect the accuracy of any assessment made, and recommends this practice. No evidence about **validity** is offered.

Using the Test

Only pencils are required. Instructions for **administration** are clear. Marking is straightforward. A **scoring** key would have been preferable to a simple list of correct answers. Built-in checks help to avoid marker errors. Calculation of standardized scores is easy; users must already know how to **interpret** results in this form.

Evaluation

The Test offers well-presented items on an interesting variety of topics, in a range of problem contexts. The Manual is well written and sensibly set out. Details of test administration and scoring are adequate; a scoring key would make scoring easier. Advice should be offered on score interpretation. This Test has been replaced by others in the *Basic Mathematics Test* series. There, tests offer some diagnostic help,as well as simply ordering pupils with respect to each other and a notional national sample.

MATHEMATICS ATTAINMENT TEST DE2

National Foundation for Educational Research
First Published 1970; Standardized 1968, 1969
NFER-NELSON, UK
10:00–11:11 (10:01–11:09)
Group
Untimed; (50 mins)
Standard Scores in one-month age bands
Consumable booklets

Item Distribution

	Number	Measurement	Space	Algebra	Logic	Statistics
Comprehension	17	5	6	3	9	–
Technique	4	3	1	1	3	–
Recall	2	–	1	–	–	–

Presentation							Response				Context		
Words	Numbers	Algebra	Figures	Graphs	Pictures	Oral	Free Format	Forced Choice	Constructed Lines	Explanation	Abstract	Concrete	Total
46	37	12	20	–	–	–	22	21	3	–	24	22	46

The *Mathematics Attainment Test* series has been replaced by the *Basic Mathematics Test* series. The detailed review of *Mathematics Attainment Test A* can be compared with the review of *Basic Mathematics Test A* in order to see the nature of the changes made. Only a brief review will be presented here.

Purposes

'to provide a test somewhat broader in context than traditional arithmetic tests ...'; 'questions were ... designed to assess mathematical understanding, rather than skill in computation.'

Content

Forty-six items are presented. These are concerned with reasoning, calculation of lengths and areas, algebra, presenting and interpreting information; patterns, fractions and choice of operation. Item format is varied, and includes a number of geometric figures and tables.

Test development

'Data were collected on the original version ... during 1968 and 1969 ... late in 1969, the modified version of the Test [including decimal currency, metric units] was given to 3541 children ...' No significant differences were found between the samples, and so the data were pooled, giving a sample size of 10,012. No information is provided about these **standardizing** samples.

> 'It is likely that the replacement questions will become progress-ively easier as children are taught, and understand, more about decimal and metric measurements. This means that the conversion table ... will probably underestimate a child's ability for a little while, although this underestimate will decrease as time goes by.'

No significant differences were found between scores of boys and girls; common norms are provided.

Reliability was assessed via KR–20 for an unspecified random sample of 241 children. The value, 0.95, corresponds to an SEM of 3.44 at age 11:00. Larger estimates of the SEM are suggested for younger and older children. The Manual explains the use of the SEM to reflect the accuracy of any measurement made.

No evidence is offered concerning **validity**.

Using the Test

Pupils require pencils and a ruler. Instructions for **administration** are clear and sensible. **Marking** is straightforward: the scoring key aligns with the test booklet, and built-in checks help avoid marker errors. Calculation of standard scores is easy and the Manual explains how they can be **interpreted** in terms of percentiles.

Evaluation

Test items are clearly presented, and offer a wide range of mathematical topics, many of which require logical thought rather than the deployment of well-learned algorithms. The Manual is well written and clearly set out; details of test administration and scoring are quite adequate. This Test has been replaced by others in the *Basic Mathematics* series.

MATHEMATICS ATTAINMENT TEST EF

National Foundation for Educational Research
First Published 1972; Standardized 1972, 1974; Manual Revised 1975
NFER-NELSON, UK
11:00–13:06 (11:01–13:01)
Group
Untimed; (50 mins)
Standard Scores in one-month age bands
Reusable booklets, consumable answer sheets; machine scorable

Item Distribution

	Number	Measurement	Space	Algebra	Logic	Statistics
Comprehension	9	4	–	3	3	3
Technique	17	4	5	1	–	–
Recall	4	–	13	–	–	–

Presentation

Words	Numbers	Algebra	Figures	Graphs	Pictures	Oral
60	51	3	17	8	–	–

Response

Free Format	Forced Choice	Constructed Lines	Explanation
–	60	–	–

Context

Abstract	Concrete	Total
22	38	60

The *Mathematics Attainment Test* series has been replaced by the *Basic Mathematics Test* series. The detailed review of *Mathematics Attainment Test A* can be compared with the review of *Basic Mathematics Test A* in order to see the nature of the changes made. Only a brief review will be presented here.

Purposes

'... to assess understanding of mathematical concepts rather than computational skills ,... in content and behaviour sampling it is similar to the other tests in the *Mathematics Attainment* series.'

Content

Sixty items involve the use of fractions, percentages, decimals, approximation, 2–D and 3–D shapes, angles, similarity, graphs, interpreting diagrams, ratio and sets as well as single and multiple digit operations. A wide range of item formats is used, including graphs, tables, geometric figures and Venn diagrams. Pupils respond by choosing a response alternative provided on a separate answer sheet.

Test development

A specification of test items 'was drawn up to reflect the present "common core" topics taught in secondary schools for the age range 11 to 13. It samples six behaviour types and five broad content categories'. The behaviour types are knowledge; techniques and skill; comprehension (translation, interpretation, extrapolation); and application. The content categories are number concepts, number operations, space, tabular/graphical representation, and geometry. These are further divided into 39 specific categories; the distribution of items within this behaviour types content matrix is shown.

Scores from 8,969 pupils aged 11 years and over, and 2,609 pupils aged 12 years and over, obtained from an unspecified sample sometime in 1972 and 1974, were used to provide *standard scores*. There were no significant differences in the scores of girls and boys aged 12+, and at age 11+ differences were considered small enough to be ignored.

'Because the samples of 11+ and 12+ pupils were found to be different in terms of both age-allowance and mean attainment level, two sets of conversion tables are provided. One set of tables must be used consistently for a particular age group.'

Reliability was assessed via KR–20 for 362 pupils in the 11+ age group, and 357 pupils in the 12+ age group. The values of 0.90 and 0.92 correspond to SEMs of 4.62 at mean age 11:10, and 4.34 at mean age 12:06, respectively. Modified SEMs are suggested for other ages, and the use of SEM to reflect the accuracy of any assessment made is described.

No evidence is offered concerning **validity**.

Using the Test

Pupils require pencils, a ruler, eraser, and scrap paper. A practice test is provided to familiarize pupils with the Test and the answer sheet. Instructions for **administration** are clear, and sensible.

Marking is straightforward; a list of answers is provided, together with a marking stencil. The stencil is used to overlay the pupil's answer sheet, and facilitates marking.

Calculation of standard scores is easy; users are advised to use the conversion table 'for which the mean age of the children tested is closest to the mean age of the standardization sample'. An **interpretation** of standardized scores in terms of percentiles is provided.

Evaluation

Test items are well presented; administration and scoring are straightforward. A strong feature of this test is that an effort has been made to design its contents logically.

Content and behaviour categories are both specified, along with a warning that the classification offered is not unique. By designing stencils, the user could derive pupil profiles on each of the behaviours and contents listed – although the reliability of such profiles would be rather low.

The analysis of the number of items in different behaviour categories shows that more than half of the questions are related to 'technique and skill'. This does not accord with the stated purpose to 'assess understanding ... rather than computational skills ...' Nevertheless, the Test is far from being a measure of algorithmic skills.

Details of the nature of the standardization sample are inadequate. This Test has been replaced by others in the *Basic Mathematics Test* series.

MORAY HOUSE MATHEMATICS TEST 7

The Godfrey Thompson Unit,
University of Edinburgh
First Published 1970; Standardized
1971; Manual Revised 1972
Hodder and Stoughton, UK
10:00–12:00 (10:00–11:05)
Group
Timed; 45 mins
Standard Scores in one-month age
bands
Consumable booklets
**May only be used with the permission
of the Chief Education Officer**

Item Distribution

	Number	Measurement	Space	Algebra	Logic	Statistics
Comprehension	43	7	5	–	18	1
Technique	9	5	–	–	5	–
Recall	–	–	–	–	–	–

Presentation						
Words	Numbers	Algebra	Figures	Graphs	Pictures	Oral
54	62	–	17	5	–	–

Response			
Free Format	Forced Choice	Constructed Lines	Explanation
60	5	–	–

Context		
Abstract	Concrete	Total
36	29	65

Purposes

None are stated, although 'It has been administered to children of ages between 10 and 12 in examinations held either to determine awards of places in grammar schools or to control promotion to other post-primary courses'.

Content

Sixty-five items focus on single and multiple digit operations, fractions, number series, reading graphs and diagrams, and logical problems. Item format is varied, with items appearing as numbers, expressed in words, or in graphs, sketch maps or geometrical diagrams.

Test development

No information is given about item preparation, nor about the authors' intentions. The Test was **standardized** on two samples (from different Education Authorities) comprising 2022 pupils. No information is provided about these samples, other than that boys and girls were represented in roughly equal proportions, and that their ages ranged from 10:00 to 11:05, and 10:02 to 11:01.

> '... performance in the test will depend on the school syllabus and on the time devoted in schools to the subject. The present conversion table, however, is based on what may be regarded as a satisfactory sample of the whole population.'

There is little to justify this assertion. Norms of 'Mathematical Quotients' (MQ) are provided for pupils aged 10:00 to 12:00 in one-month age bands even though the standardization sample only extended to 11:05. No warnings are given about the dangers of extrapolation, and users are told how to extrapolate MQs for pupils aged up to 12:06 and down to 9:06. MQs above 140 and below 70 are to be recorded as 140+ and 70−, respectively.

A mean raw score difference of 2.3 points in favour of boys was found; separate norms are provided for boys and girls. '... For purposes of transfer to secondary schools it is recommended that the sexes be considered independently of each other ...'

The mean score was 21.6 out of a possible 65 marks, reflecting the relative difficulty of this test for pupils, and its potential for discriminating amongst high− rather than low-attaining pupils.

Reliability was assessed by calculating KR–20 for 201 scripts; this was found to be 0.96.

The only information concerning **validity** is provided by correlations with a Moray House Test of Verbal Reasoning (0.89), and of English (0.81). This information suggests that some general intellectual competence is involved, but provides no evidence about the validity of this Test as a measure of mathematical ability.

Using the Test

Two supervisors should be present, if possible. Pencils and a stopwatch (or wristwatch) should be available; rulers, erasers and scrap paper should not. Details of test **administration** are explicit and clear. Pupils are told the time at 15 minute intervals, and the script for administration is quite adequate.

The **scoring key** is easy to use; the Manual recommends that each script be double-marked. Built-in checks help the scorer to avoid errors. Standardized scores are easy to find from the table; users would be unwise to place much faith in MQs extrapolated for older or younger children via the formula provided. An **interpretation** of MQ in terms of percentiles is offered.

Evaluation

Test items are quite interesting, and cover a reasonable range of mathematical topics, including a good deal of reasoning. The details of test administration and scoring are clear, and completely adequate.

Details about the standardization sample are quite inadequate; the cavalier approach to the extrapolation of MQs to older and younger children cannot be justified. The absence of any statement about possible uses for the Test, or about the origins of test items gives cause for concern. So, too, does the idea that LEAs might use such a test as the basis for secondary school selection, without reference to the different primary school curriculae followed. The score distribution suggests that the Test has been developed to discriminate amongst high-attaining pupils, rather than across the ability range.

NOTTINGHAM NUMBER TEST

W.E.C. Gillham and K.A. Hesse
First Published 1973; Standardized
1972
Hodder and Stoughton, UK
9:01–11:00 (9:01–11:00)
Group
Untimed; (55 mins)
Standard Scores in one-year age
bands; Percentiles; some diagnostic
use
Consumable booklets

Item Distribution

	Number	Measurement	Space	Algebra	Logic	Statistics
Comprehension	10	–	–	–	10	–
Technique	51	2	6	–	–	–
Recall	18	–	–	–	–	–

Presentation

Words	Numbers	Algebra	Figures	Graphs	Pictures	Oral
44	85	–	19	–	–	88

Response

Free Format	Forced Choice	Constructed Lines	Explanation
77	11	–	–

Context

Abstract	Concrete	Total
78	10	88

Purposes

The Test is 'intended for the top two years of the junior school, to be given at the beginning of the school year.'

'... it aims to measure children's developing grasp of our base-ten number system.'

'separate norms are provided (for number concept scores and skill scores) ... for diagnostic purposes ...'

'Our ... test is aimed at assessing what is considered essential in any mathematics programme.'

'The test is designed:
a) to indicate areas of weakness in individual children;
b) to provide a basis for grouping for teaching;
c) to detect gross educational failure as part of a comprehensive attainment assessment programme;
d) to make possible, in conjunction with the *Leicester Number Test* a continuous appraisal of attainment in number through the junior school;
e) to give some guidance as to the content and emphasis of an essential part of primary school mathematics.'

'To provide a more precise discrimination amongst the bottom 25 per cent of the age groups – and more sensitively record their progress.'

Content

The 43 items produce scores on two scales: Number Concepts and Number Skills. The Number Concepts scale consists mainly of items concerned with place value, counting and knowledge of fractions, with a few items concerned with ordering, extending patterns, writing down numbers spoken aloud, and operations on multiple digits. Most items present numbers or shapes; a few present familiar objects, a number line, or simply space to write responses to oral questions. The Number Skills scale consists mainly of operations on multiple digit numbers, on decimals, and on fractions; there are two other items on operations on single digits. All the items present numbers to pupils, and pupils respond mainly by writing numbers.

Easy practice items are presented to raise curiosity and arouse motivation. The first 20 items of the Test are all easy. The Test is presented orally, to avoid reading difficulties, and instructions are clear.

Test Development

The Schools Council publication *Mathematics in Primary Schools* (HMSO, 1965) was used to determine the content of the Number Concepts scale; addition of the Number Skills scale was justified by survey data that showed that over 95 per cent of schoolchildren had begun formal written arithmetic by the age of 7:06. Number Concepts focus on place value and series. Number Skills refer to the use of basic operations on integers, decimals and fractions.

The authors attempted to provide 'adequate and balanced representation of ... concepts and skills ... as well as adequate representation of different levels of difficulty.' No information is provided about how items were selected.

The Test was **standardized** 'on a representative sample of non-immigrant children in the City of Nottingham' in September 1972. It was readministered a week later so that the test-retest reliability could be assessed. The standard scores presented are based on 264 boys and 245 girls in their third year and 253 boys and 263 girls in their fourth year, from schools in each quadrant of the city; no other information is provided about the sampling procedure. The authors claim that in 1963 'social-class composition of the City closely resembles the national pattern', but warn that there might have been 'some movement of middle-class families to surburban areas' by the time the Test was standardized.

The raw score distribution of the Number Skills scale is positively skewed, as is the full scale score distribution for third-year pupils; the authors' intentions to discriminate amongst low-attaining pupils have not, therefore, been fulfilled. Further, the mean performances are rather low: for example, mean scores on Number Skills for third years and fourth years are 13 and 17.5 respectively, out of 44. Standard scores (called 'quotients') are presented for each year band (9:01 to 10:00; 10:01 to 11:00) together with percentile scores. No age allowance is made, and no information is presented about sex differences.

Test-retest **reliability** based on 472 third years was found to be 0.94 for the whole test, corresponding to an SEM of 3.6 points; for the 483 fourth years it was 0.96, corresponding to an SEM of 3.0. Test-retest reliabilities for the subscales were acceptably high, the worst being 0.91.

The Manual asserts that the Test samples what is taught, and therefore 'satisfactory validity essentially follows from satisfactory reliability'. The labels on the subscales 'are essentially descriptive and the separate scores are highly correlated'. The concurrent **validity** of the Test was assessed by comparing test scores with teacher ranks of pupils' understanding of number and proficiency in written arithmetic. A single school took part, and teachers had known pupils for a whole school year. Pupils were tested again 12 weeks later. Spearman's *rho* was calculated (on unspecified numbers of children) to be between 0.54 and 0.87, which is considered 'satisfactory for this type of measure'. It is hard to interpret this evidence.

Using the Test

The Test is **administered** orally, and is untimed. It should be used by a teacher with some skill in test administration, together with an invigilator if possible; a trial run with another group is recommended. Spare pencils and a stopwatch are needed. The Manual offers good advice on classroom organization and testing practices and points out some of the difficulties of administering tests orally; the script for administration is clear. The administrator must judge when each child has finished.

Instructions for **scoring** are unambiguous and sensible. No separate scoring key is provided, and so the marker must cross-check between the answer sheet and the Manual. Spaces are provided on the answer sheets for marks clearly identified as items on either the Number Concept or Number Skills scales.

A raw score is calculated, which is converted to a standard score and a percentile. These are reported as numbers, rather than as score bands. An interpretation of the SEM is described in the Manual, and this SEM should have been incorporated into each pupil's score.

Interpretation of results is direct, and might form a basis for the purposes a) and c) above, and perhaps b); but not, in my view, for purposes d) and e) (for the reasons set out below).

Evaluation

The Test aims to assess what is considered essential in any primary mathematics classroom. It fails in these aims because of the datedness and the difficulty of its content. Little of the content of the Test seems related to contemporary primary mathematics curricula; the norms are therefore likely to be of little use, since they derive from pupils who studied different aspects of mathematics.

The choice of items seems hard to justify. Few items are devoted to ordering, and none to measurement. A very narrow range of contexts is used; no items relate to time or money or to other 'realistic' situations. Children aged between 9:00 and 11:00 are asked to add, subtract, multiply and divide fractions and decimal numbers (involving three places of decimals on occasions) and to engage in long division. Of the eight items involving number skills or fractions, none involve addition or subtraction with 'easy' denominators such as two, four, eight or 16; four require multiplication and division. A cursory inspection of the items shows they will be far too hard for the intended age groups. An examination of the distribution of scores confirms this view: only one per cent of the pupils get more than 75 per cent of the available marks on the Number Skills test; median scores, out of a possible 88, are 33 for third years and 46 for fourth years. It hardly seems useful to offer pupils and teachers the view that such tasks reflect relevant number concepts for them, or to expose pupils to failure on very hard tasks which apparently reflect mathematical attainment. The main use of the Test seems to be to discriminate between very high-attaining pupils on the basis of 'hard sums'. Far more attention should have been paid to the choice of operations and the range of numbers they are applied to.

If the Test is to have any conceptual or diagnostic use, users must decide for themselves on the content validity of each item. Scores on scales labelled 'concepts' and 'skills' are of little use on their own. Test design would probably have been helped by actively spelling out the number skills and concepts required to solve each item (and might have helped balance the content better); users would certainly have found such analysis useful.

The Manual is well presented and well written; instructions for using the Test are clear.

NUMBER TEST DE

E.L. Barnard
First Published 1970; Standardized
1965
NFER-NELSON, UK
10:06–12:06 (10:08–12:03)
Group
Untimed; (50 mins)
Standard Scores in one-month age
bands
Consumable booklets

Item Distribution

	Number	Measurement	Space	Algebra	Logic	Statistics
Comprehension	39	–	6	–	14	–
Technique	1	–	–	14	–	–
Recall	–	–	–	–	–	–

Presentation						
Words	Numbers	Algebra	Figures	Graphs	Pictures	Oral
44	48	36	10	–	–	–

Response			
Free Format	Forced Choice	Constructed Lines	Explanation
32	18	–	1

Context		
Abstract	Concrete	Total
44	6	50

Purposes

'... to provide a measure of the child's understanding of the four
number processes ...'

'... a child who "understood" these processes would be able to
use them as a basis from which to generalize and draw
inferences.'

Content

The Test aims to assess knowledge of the basic number operations
in a variety of unfamiliar contexts. In 50 items, single and multiple

digit operations are presented, along with items on fractions and number bases, and series. Some questions require algebraic manipulation. Numbers and operations are often coded as geometric symbols, which pupils have to interpret before using their number skills.

Test development

The author's intentions are clear (see *Purposes*). No information is given about early trials. In the Summer Term of 1965, 855 third-year, and 2329 fourth-year Juniors from two small urban LEAs took the Test. It was judged to be too hard for the third years (less than half of whom scored more than 12 out of a possible 50 marks). These pupils were excluded from the **standardizing** sample. In the Autumn Term of 1965, 3398 children in their first year of secondary education in a County LEA took the Test. These data were pooled with that from the fourth-year Juniors in the preparation of standardized scores. An adequate raw score distribution was produced. No information is provided about the nature of these standardizing samples. Differences between scores of boys and girls when corrected for age were not significantly different, nor were the regression slopes of score and age. Therefore a single table of standard scores is provided, in one-month age bands. Scores for pupils aged 12:04 to 12:06 have been extrapolated.

Test-retest **reliability**, assessed via KR–20, was found to be 0.96, corresponding to an SEM of 2.84 at age 11:06. The Manual suggests larger values for extreme ages.

Concurrent **validity** was assessed by comparison of scores with other tests taken at the same time, and with teachers' order of merit lists, for the scores of 804 fourth years; $r = 0.84$. '... If one can assume that the teachers were able to rank the children truly by their "understanding of number processes" (rather than by their skill in computation) then the test can be said to be associated with this aspect of mathematics.' The correlation with the NFER *Intermediate Diagnostic Arithmetic Test 1* was 0.85 for third– and fourth–year juniors. This value is probably inflated by the large ability spread.

Correlations with raw scores from 113 secondary modern schoolchildren were the *NFER Verbal Test EF* (0.86); *Schonell*

Essential Intelligence (Verbal) (0.76); *Schonell Problem Arithmetic* (0.70); *Schonell Mechanical Arithmetic* (0.64); teachers' scaled order of merit (0.62); *Schonell Graded Word Reading* (0.55); *NFER Non-Verbal Test DH* (0.57).

Using the Test

Pencils and scrap paper are required. The details of test **administration**, and the examiner's script are sensible, and well set-out. **Scoring** is simple: an easy-to-use scoring key is provided, though it could be improved further by repositioning some of the answers. One item requires pupils to describe 'halving' in words – no less than 16 alternative wordings are offered! (Although this does not detract from the worth of the activity.) Internal checks help avoid marker errors.

Standard scores are presented in one-month age bands, and are easy to derive. The Manual explains the use of the SEM in **interpreting** scores.

Evaluation

The Test sets out to assess understanding of the basic number operations by setting them in unfamiliar contexts. These contexts usually involve pupils in understanding and using symbol systems before they can demonstrate their number skills; a good deal of careful reading, logical analysis and reasoning appears to be involved in the Test. All the activities described are worthwhile mathematically, but some users may question their dominance in a 'number test'. Little or no attention is paid to aspects of the *deployment* of number skills, such as the mastery of the technique of base 10 number work. No attempt is made to assess pupils' ability to deploy number skills in 'realistic' contexts such as shopping, travel or hobbies (where technique can be combined with decision about the choice of operation to employ). (The extent to which number skills generalize across the rather abstract items presented here, to mundane contexts, is of course an interesting empirical question.)

Anyone interested in exploring pupils' understanding of number should consider using this test. Most of the items would form the basis for pupil explanations of number work and for group and class discussions about a variety of aspects of number. With more work, it could form the basis for the diagnosis and remediation of misconceptions in this area.

Test items are interesting, details of administration and scoring are clear and the Manual is well written. Too little information is presented, however, about the nature of the standardizing sample.

PROFILE OF MATHEMATICAL SKILLS

Norman France
First Published 1979; Standardized 1978
NFER-NELSON, UK
8:00–15:00 (8:04–14:09)
Group
Untimed
Standard Scores in six-month age bands; Profiles, Percentiles; Stanines; diagnostic
Consumable booklets

LEVEL I
Item Distribution

	Number	Measurement	Space	Algebra	Logic	Statistics
Comprehension	47	10	4	–	6	–
Technique	113	8	11	4	–	–
Recall	1	10	–	–	–	–

Presentation						
Words	Numbers	Algebra	Figures	Graphs	Pictures	Oral
80	188	4	19	4	–	–

Response			
Free Format	Forced Choice	Constructed Lines	Explanation
155	33	–	–

Context		
Abstract	Concrete	Total
125	63	188

LEVEL 2
Item Distribution

	Number	Measurement	Space	Algebra	Logic	Statistics
Comprehension	52	12	12	4	4	–
Technique	136	20	4	–	–	–
Recall	–	8	–	–	–	–

Presentation						
Words	Numbers	Algebra	Figures	Graphs	Pictures	Oral
126	228	4	30	4	–	–

Response			
Free Format	Forced Choice	Constructed Lines	Explanation
199	33	–	–

Context		
Abstract	Concrete	Total
137	95	232

Purposes

'... essentially a criterion-referenced test ... for which pupils' achievement on the criteria have been established and measured.'

'... provides a diagnostic assessment of the individual pupil's abilities and skills ... in the various areas of mathematical understanding ... and ... allows the teacher to discover the nature of specific weaknesses which may be retarding progress...'

'measures depth of understanding and not speed of working.'

'... the teacher obtains an immediate and valid picture of the pupil's relative strengths and weaknesses in ... different ... mathematical skills and abilities.'

'An analysis of the class results ... provides the teacher with valuable guidance as to how the balance of mathematical teaching needs to be adjusted to remedy any common class weakness found.'

The Pupil Profile Chart 'may be of value to teachers in a variety of contexts including
record-keeping procedures;
discussions with colleagues;
discussions with parents;
transfer of information as pupils change schools.'

Content

The *Profile* focuses on two levels: Level 1 relates directly to third-year junior school pupils; Level 2 relates directly to second-year secondary school pupils 'but, in addition, each Level has been standardized on three consecutive year groups for continuity...'
    Level 1 assesses addition, subtraction, multiplication, division, choice of operation, measurement and money; Level 2 assesses each of these, and also fractions, decimal fractions and percentages, and diagrams.

Test development

In 1977, as an initial trial, a pool of 256 items was administered to about 2000 children aged between nine and 13 years, at schools in Doncaster, Wolverhampton and Leeds. This trial allowed items to be selected for the final edition 'in ascending and equal grades of difficulty, and to discriminate efficiently within the full ability range in the appropriate year groups.'
    Standardization took place in June 1978 and involved 8220 pupils in a national sample that was 'fully representative of the United Kingdom school population'. Between 1300 and 1400 children were tested in each of the six year groups. In addition, a supplementary group in middle schools were tested using both Levels, which enabled Standard Age scores between Levels 1 and 2 derived from the larger sample to be verified.

Overall, the spread of raw scores was higher for boys than for girls. The small superiority of girls in junior school gradually declined and was reversed in the third year of secondary school. '... the superiority of girls over boys was slightly greater for the tests of mathematical skills and slightly less for the tests involving reasoning and spatial abilities.' Regional differences in raw score were rather small, although the Midlands region produced a greater spread of scores.

Scores from one-sixth of the pupils, chosen at random, were analysed in greater detail to provide evidence on test reliability, and the structure of the tests. **Reliability** was assessed either by split half correlation, or by KR–21 for each subtest in each year. Median reliability was 0.87; the lowest value found was 0.68. When the Test as a whole is considered, reliabilities of 0.98 for Level 1 (based on 188 items) and 0.99 for Level 2 (based on 232 items) are reported. These are remarkably high. The Manual provides a table which relates reliability coefficients to the SEM.

There are three sources of information about **validity**. The Manual provides an item-by-item description of the content of each subtest, so that surface validity can be inspected directly. Teachers were asked to rate pupils' mathematical ability and mathematical skill, in order to examine concurrent validity. The two teacher estimates were highly correlated (0.95). When these estimates were correlated with pupil performance on the whole battery of subtests the values (0.63 to 0.73 in junior school; 0.29 to 0.51 in secondary school) were 'lower than one would have expected'.

A factor analysis, using each subtest score at each level, produced five factors which accounted for about 90 per cent of the total variance. The factors were interpreted to be mathematical and spatial reasoning; addition; multiplication; division (at Level 1) or operational (at Level 2); and teacher/pupil interaction. These data offer some evidence about construct validity, but do not fully support the choice of seven subtests in the profile (which might, in any case, be justified on conceptual grounds alone).

Using the Test

Details of test **administration** take the form of suggestions rather than instructions: the purpose of testing is to be explained to pupils, and testing is to take place in an informal atmosphere. No more than one subtest should be given in the same lesson; children can be given different subtests to avoid copying.

Scoring involves the use of a scoring key which has a similar spatial layout to the pupil's answer sheet for each of the subtests; a good deal of careful cross-checking is required. Correct answers are totalled and transferred to the front of the booklet, by ringing an appropriate number. Ringed scores are then connected, to provide the pupil's profile.

Interpretation is direct. The Manual describes standard scores (Standard Age scores) in terms of both percentages and stanines; it also explains the meaning of mathematical ages, and advises caution in their use.

'The tests of mathematical skills such as addition, subtraction, multiplication, division and operations are designed to be most effective at and below the average level of ability in order to produce the most useful diagnosis of individual difficulties in the mastery of these basic skills. On the other hand, the remaining tests, involving mathematical and spatial reasoning ability, are intended to measure inequalities of more advanced development, particularly for the average and better than average pupil.'

Errors of measurement are discussed. Special attention should be paid to pupils whose profiles show marked differences in attainment on different subtests. The Manual warns against the dangers of over-interpreting small differences in subtest scores (less than 15 points). A pupil summary is available to allow the educational progress of each pupil to be monitored over five successive tests.

Scores are not viewed as replacements for professional judgement:

'The best assessment derives from the long acquaintance that an experienced teacher has with the individual child. It is when these two prerequisites ... are missing that the value of an authoritative estimate of mathematical ability and skill ... will be fully demonstrated.'

Teachers are also recommended to prepare a profile of the whole class performance in order to discover skills which show relative weakness. This should be followed by yet more detailed analysis of items within particular subtests, in order to discover those skills which should be the focus of further exploration and practice (via the item content descriptions provided).

Evaluation

The profile is designed to diagnose pupil strengths and weaknesses in particular mathematical skills; to pinpoint problems quite exactly; to monitor pupil progress; identify areas where the whole class can benefit from improvement; and to act as a focus for discussion with pupils, parents, colleagues and teachers in other schools. On the range of skills chosen, it seems capable of being used for all these functions.

Test development was exemplary. It included extensive pre-trialling of items; the use of large, nationally-representative standardization samples; full descriptions of items; discussion of errors of measurement; scoring and recording schemes that are quite easy to use; and a well-written, informative Manual: these are all to be commended. I was able to find only a single, unimportant error in all of the 420 items and answers – a clear sign of the care taken in test preparation.

The author states clearly that testing is meant to *support*, rather than *replace* professional judgement, and also that testing is an aid to the educational process, rather than an end in itself.

The Test focuses heavily on technical skills, with approximately half of the items on Level 1 and about one third of the items on Level 2 being devoted to technical skills on the four basic operations. These skills are undoubtedly important, but are perhaps overemphasised at the expense of a wider range of mathematical topics. Nevertheless, the *Profile* can be recommended to users who are satisfied with the range and balance of mathematical skills assessed.

RICHMOND TESTS OF BASIC SKILLS

A.N Hieronymus, E.F. Lindquist, and Norman France
First Published: Test 1974; Manuals 1975; Standardized 1974
NFER-NELSON, UK
Junior:
  Second year (Level 1) 8:01 – 9:00 (8:01 – 9:00)
  Third year (Level 2) 9:01 – 10:00 (9:01 – 10:00)
  Fourth year (Level 3) 10:01 – 11:00 (10:01 – 11:00)
Secondary:
  First year (Level 4) 11:01 – 12:00 (11:01 – 12:00)
  Second year (Level 5) 12:01 – 13:00 (12:01 – 13:00)
  Third year (Level 6) 13:01 – 14:00 (13:01 – 14:00)
Group
Timed: *Work Study Skills*, 85 mins; *Mathematics Skills*, 65 mins
Standard Scores in six-month age bands; Percentiles; Stanines; Profiles; some
diagnostic use
Reusable booklets; machine scorable sheets

MAP READING AND
READING GRAPHS
AND TABLES

Item Distribution

	Number	Measurement	Space	Algebra	Logic	Statistics
Comprehension	23	71	68	–	–	–
Technique	–	17	22	–	–	–
Recall	–	–	–	–	–	–

Presentation						
Words	Numbers	Algebra	Figures	Graphs	Pictures	Oral
161	102	–	128	33	–	–

Response			
Free Format	Forced Choice	Constructed Lines	Explanation
–	161	–	–

Context		
Abstract	Concrete	Total
0	161	161

MATHEMATICS CONCEPTS AND
MATHEMATICS PROBLEM SOLVING
Item Distribution

	Number	Measurement	Space	Algebra	Logic	Statistics
Comprehension	132	6	13	6	6	–
Technique	43	4	6	9	–	–
Recall	10	1	6	–	1	–

Presentation						
Words	Numbers	Algebra	Figures	Graphs	Pictures	Oral
232	221	15	59	1	–	–

Response			
Free Format	Forced Choice	Constructed Lines	Explanation
–	232	–	–

Context		
Abstract	Concrete	Total
76	156	232

Purposes

The Tests
'... provide for the comprehensive and continuous measurement of the growth of an individual child in the fundamental skills: vocabulary, reading, language, methods of study, and mathematics.'
'... help the teacher to discover what subskills a particular pupil (or class) has not mastered, and possibly to spot deficiencies in the learning materials or the teaching approach.'
'Periodic, reliable measurement of the development of these skills provides an incentive to the pupil, a tool for the teacher, a guide for the school, and an accounting to the parents.'
'... of crucial worth ... in the provision of "bridging" information as children move from one level of schooling to the next.'
'... facilitate provision for individual differences in needs and abilities.'

Content

The Richmond Tests of Basic Skills comprise 11 separate tests, each assessed at six levels. There is a good deal of overlap between levels. Tests are grouped into five categories: Vocabulary; Reading Comprehension; Language Skills; Work-Study Skills; and Mathematics Skills. Work Study Skills and Mathematics Skills are the focus of this review.

The skills classification for both Mathematics Concepts and Mathematics Problem Solving lists currency; decimals; equations, inequalities and number sentences; fractions; geometry; measurement; numeration and number systems; percentages; ratio and proportion; sets; and whole numbers. There are 136 items in all, spread over six levels for Concepts, and 96 items for Problem Solving.

Work Study Skills are assessed in the same testing session via three subtests Map Reading (89 items), Reading Graphs and Tables (74 items), and Knowledge and Use of Reference Materials.

All the Tests are presented in a single booklet and each pupil takes a Test set at a level appropriate to their educational development. Within each category, time limits and test directions are the same for each test level permitting the simultaneous administration of Tests at different levels, if necessary.

The *Teacher's Guide* offers, for each subtest, a description and classification of the skills involved; a categorization of each item in terms of this skills list, and suggestions for classroom activities to develop these skills.

Test development

These Tests were developed from the *Iowa Tests of Basic Skills*. The content was 'very carefully modified to represent the British environment and current curriculum practice ...'

'Items ... have been selected to represent certain classes of *skills*. Each of these skills represents a behavioural objective which could have been stated in a more formal manner.'

'The main criteria for determining each skills classification system are *meaningfulness* and *usefulness* to the teacher in describing behaviour for which the school accepts responsibility.'

A trial in 1974 involved 700 children in 24 classes in primary and secondary school; this provided data for item analyses, and on the discrimination power of each item for each level of the tests. Tests were modified before being administered to a **standardization** sample which consisted of 'A national sample, thoroughly prepared and weighted as necessary to reflect school types and socioeconomic population distribution ... in England, Wales, Scotland and Northern Ireland'. The *Teacher's Guide* claims that 17,000 children took part; the table of norms refers to 'over 12,000' children, and the total weighted sample size is 16,096! For each year band, sample size varied between 1,600 and 2,300 pupils. Testing took place in October and November, 1974.

Reliability was calculated via KR–21 for each subtest; values ranged overall from 0.71 on Map Reading, to 0.89 on Mathematical Concepts. The Manual provides a table which relates these reliability coefficients to likely measurement errors. 'The validity of any test is a function of the extent to which it represents objectives of instruction. The behaviour called for in the Test should correspond as nearly as possible to the behaviour called for in the objectives.' There are no descriptions of how the tests have been used, or of how test scores compare with scores on other tests, or any information related to **validity**.

Using the Tests

Details of the preparations for testing are clear; so too are details of test **administration**. Pupils require booklets, rough paper, HB pencils and soft erasers. The administrator needs some method for accurate timing.

Tests are machine **scorable**. The directions for coding the pupils' names into a machine-readable form may well be too difficult for less able, or younger children to follow, and may best be done by the teacher (who is advised to check each form, in any case). Tests can also be scored manually via transparent overlays, which are easy to use. Norms provide standard scores (called Standard Age scores) in six-month age bands; tables also allow users to derive percentiles and stanine scores. The Manual explains the derivation and meaning of each of these scores.

Individual pupil profiles can be prepared. The table of norms warns against overemphasising differences in standard scores on different subtests; nevertheless, in the examples given, it commits just this error. A class record sheet is provided, which can be used to record the raw score and standard score of each pupil on each subtest.

A good deal of advice is offered on score **interpretation**. The *Teacher's Guide* contains a section headed 'Use of Test Results in Improving Instruction'.

> 'Tests are aids to better instruction ... the usefulness of tests will depend upon the extent to which the test results are interpreted with wisdom, ingenuity, and caution. Test results should be used to supplement, not to replace, teacher judgement. They should be used in conjunction with everything else the teacher knows about the pupil to meet his instructional needs.'

Standard scores can be used to monitor each pupil's 'rate of development' with respect to peers. The derivation of a pupil profile may prove of value when pupils change class, or schools, and should offer guidance on individual strengths and weaknesses.

A description of each item is provided in terms of the skills which it tests. Teachers are recommended to examine the list of skills, and to 'think about the extent to which provisions have been made for the development of these skills'. Suggestions are made for teaching techniques which might foster the skills assessed by each subtest.

Analysis of the performance of the whole class can be used to identify topics in need of further coverage. Teachers are advised to specify, in advance of testing, the proportion of the class who should respond correctly to each item, and to revise topics where performance is below expectation. This procedure is actually far harder than it sounds; it is rather hard to guess how difficult different items will prove to be. Examination of responses to individual items may provide clues to specific pupil difficulties. These should be explored via teacher-made test items.

Evaluation

The status given to understanding and inference under the heading 'Basic Skills' is to be applauded. The emphasis throughout the

Manual is that 'tests are aids to better instruction ...' is also welcome. So, too, is the description of the behaviours which each item attempts to assess, and the teaching suggestions which accompany them. Most of the items in Map Reading, and Reading Graphs and Tables, are interesting intellectual challenges which require a good deal of reflection and analysis – far more than one would normally find in conventional books or tests in mathematics. In contrast, Mathematics Problem Solving presents a collection of rather unimaginative word problems; Mathematics Concepts seems to present more novel challenges, and to require more understanding.

The choice of contents sampled by the *Richmond Tests of Basic Skills* as a whole seems somewhat strange: vocabulary, spelling, use of capital letters and punctuation are all assessed via their own subtest. By implication, each of these skills is seen to be as important as Mathematics Concepts and Mathematical Problem Solving.

The Manual fails to provide data on intercorrelations between subtests; correlations with other tests, or any evidence that the subtests do assess what they claim. Nor is evidence presented about Levels: it becomes clear that they reflect steadily increasing difficulty, rather than qualitative leaps in performance or understanding. The advice that profiles should not be over-interpreted is sound, but the Manual would have been improved by estimates of the score differences which are, and are not, noteworthy. It would also have been helpful if the Manual had not ignored its own good advice in its illustrative descriptions of pupil scores.

Too many of the suggestions for developing skills in mathematics are phrased as general advice, unlike the specific suggestions found elsewhere: for example compare 'create a climate in which the importance of mathematics is recognized ...' with 'give pupils practice in tracing great circle routes on the globe' offered in Map Reading.

From the sole viewpoint of the assessment of mathematical attainment, the *Richmond Tests* provide some challenging items (albeit not formally within the subtests focused on mathematics) but are, generally, too thinly spread for detailed monitoring of mathematical performance.

SENIOR MATHEMATICS TEST

National Foundation for Educational Research
First Published 1963; Standardized 1975; Manual Revised 1976
NFER-NELSON, UK
16:00–18:00 (16:00–17:11)
Group
Timed; 45 mins
Standard Scores in one-month age bands
Consumable booklets

Item Distribution

	Number	Measurement	Space	Algebra	Logic	Statistics
Comprehension	8	–	13	1	7	–
Technique	14	–	1	12	3	1
Recall	–	–	1	–	–	–

Presentation						
Words	Numbers	Algebra	Figures	Graphs	Pictures	Oral
30	43	14	11	–	–	–

Response			
Free Format	Forced Choice	Constructed Lines	Explanation
49	–	–	1

Context		
Abstract	Concrete	Total
25	25	50

Purposes

'… to assess the mathematical attainment level of general entry groups in Colleges of Further Education. It is intended for use in allocation to the various courses available, particularly those in the more technical subjects.'

Content

Fifty items cover a spread of topics, including algebra, geometry, operations on fractions and decimals, ratio and percentage. Few items deal with straightforward multiple-digit operations. No less than 10 items present geometric figures: many present problems algebraically or in words.

Test development

No information is given about the origin of items (which resemble standard textbook questions) or about any early trials which may have been carried out. 'The test was **standardized** using a sample of engineering student entrants in (October) 1975 ... It must be stressed that the colleges providing the data were those agreeing to co-operate with the NFER and there is no guarantee that they are representative.' 1340 students, aged 16:00 to 17:11 took part; most of them were male, and so only norms for males are provided. Standard Scores are provided in one-month age bands.

Reliability was assessed via KR–20 and was found to be 0.95 for an unspecified sample of 352 students. This corresponds to an SEM of 3.3 standard score points. The Manual explains how this SEM is to be used to interpret student scores.

No information is provided about the **validity** of the Test. The Manual offers 'a breakdown of the mean scores for groups on various courses' such as Electrical, Construction, Mechanical and Motor Vehicle Engineering, often for quite small (less than 100) numbers of students. No uses are suggested for these data; indeed, it is hard to think of any.

Using the Test

Two invigilators should **administer** the Test. A stopwatch, and pencils are required. Advice on test administration is sensible and clear; the supervisor's script is perfectly adequate; students are told when they have 20 minutes left to work. A **scoring** key is provided which makes scoring easy: allowable alternatives are clearly specified.

One or two features could be improved, notably the removal of alternative forms of writing units (such as sq cm, cm^2), when units are already printed on students' answer sheets; the writing of fractions in their correct form; and the correction of the erroneous answer given to Question 25. Some provisions are made to avoid marker errors. Page totals (right and wrong) are transferred to the front sheet, and totalled. Derivation of standard scores is straightforward.

The Manual explains briefly how standard scores can be **interpreted** in terms of percentiles; no advice is given concerning actions which could be taken on the basis of test results.

Evaluation

The Test was developed in 1963, and its content is therefore dated. Items are reminiscent of aged textbooks. No statement about the underlying rationale is presented for their choice, although there are clear foci on basic geometry, algebra, and the use of decimals and fractions, all of which are topics plausibly related to success on technical courses in Further Education.

As it stands, it is quite unsuitable 'for use in allocation to the various courses available' other than to act as a barrier to entry to students who perform badly. Grouping scores as test items together under broad content categories might help diagnose student strengths and weaknesses, and could form the basis for a remedial programme: but no such suggestions are made in the Manual.

Details of the standardizing sample are inadequate; the norms are unlikely to be representative of the population of interest to the user. Details about the administration of the Test, scoring, and the derivation of standard scores are all well presented, and easy to use.

SRA ARITHMETIC INDEX

Developed by SRA Industrial Test Development Staff; Manual by Bruce A. Campbell
First Published 1968; Standardization date unspecified; Manual Revised 1974
Science Research Associates, USA
Adults and young people over 14 years (not stated)
Group
Untimed; (25 mins)
Percentiles; Criterion referenced
Consumable booklets

Item Distribution

	Number	Measurement	Space	Algebra	Logic	Statistics
Comprehension	7	–	–	–	–	–
Technique	47	–	–	–	–	–
Recall	–	–	–	–	–	–

Presentation								Response					Context		
Words	Numbers	Algebra	Figures	Graphs	Pictures	Oral		Free Format	Forced Choice	Constructed Lines	Explanation		Abstract	Concrete	Total
54	7	–	–	–	–	–		–	54	–	–		53	1	54

Purposes

This Test is one half of the *SRA Reading and Arithmetic Indexes*; the *Reading Index* will not be reviewed here.

Many jobs require little or no competence in either reading or arithmetic, yet many proficiency tests require skills in either or both of these domains. The result is that employers may reject applicants who are qualified in terms of the actual job to be performed. The *SRA Reading and Arithmetic Indexes* are designed to offer a method of 'evaluating the basic skill levels' of 'previously unqualified job applicants ... so that they can be placed in appropriate jobs'. The Tests also offer 'a means of classifying trainees by functional level in order to make the teaching sessions most effective'.

The Tests assess 'computational achievement for adults and for young people over fourteen years of age. They were designed to use with applicants for entry-level jobs and special training programs, where the basic skills of the applicants are often too low to be reliably evaluated by typical section tests.'

'... permits the user to make a rather direct comparison between the applicant's proficiency and the reading or arithmetic activities required by a job.'

'... designed for use as power tests rather than as speeded tests, since speeded tests work a hardship on individuals unfamiliar with test taking. The *RAI* [*Reading and Arithmetic Index*] indicates the maximum performance an individual is capable of, rather than the rate at which that person is able to perform.'

Content

The Test measures technical skill in arthmetic. Four 'levels' are identified: addition and subtraction of whole numbers; multiplication and division of whole numbers; basic operations involving fractions; and basic operations involving decimals and percentages. Scores on each can be derived; a wide range of difficulty is spanned, from minimum proficiency levels through to simple word problems involving percentages.

Test development

226 items, structured by item type into a four-stage hierarchy of difficulty, were pre-tested by grouping them into 18 trial units, with overlapping items. These were given to samples of students (sample size 125 to 218) of ages seven, nine, 11, 13 and 15 years. Items were chosen for the final form in order to 'maximise reliability of measurement within skill level and to provide at least a 15-point difference in the mean proportion of students passing the items at each successive level.'

Raw score frequencies and percentiles are shown for two samples as a means of offering some **standardization**: one consisting of 57 students in a Chicago training programme; the other of 419 students in Colorado and South Carolina special education programmes. Neither sample is described adequately – for example, the larger sample is aggregated from two sets, one which finished school at an average age of 13:07, the other at an average of 14:04 years. Tabulated data from these samples are quite different and no attempt is made to pool them. No data are presented on sex differences, or differences in schooling, age, or race.

Reliability was assessed via KR–20 for these two groups. The values of 0.91 for the Chicago group, and 0.95 for the Colorado-Carolina group cannot be judged without detailed information about the samples. Nevertheless, it would be surprising if a test with such a narrow focus on technical skill had a low reliability.

One approach to construct **validity** is to check that the designers' intentions about the hierarchy of levels is borne out. Of the 57 Chicago students taking the index, only four failed at one level but passed at a higher one; data for the larger sample should have been provided, too.

The correlation between the *SRA Reading Index* and *Arithmetic Index*, based on only 57 people, was found to be 0.46; the correlation with the *SRA Pictorial Reasoning Test* was 0.23. Again, data from the larger sample were, presumably, available, and should have been shown. The Manual also shows that intercorrelations between this Test and several others, for 18 occupational groups. The highest correlations were found with the *Flanagan Industrial Test-Arithmetic* (median 0.63) and with the *SRA Verbal Test* (median 0.61).

An extensive study of concurrent validity was carried out between 1969 and 1971, by correlating 'overall job ranking' and score on the *Arithmetic Index* for 18 occupations, grouped as semiskilled and unskilled; skilled, office and technical. Correlations were low, but often statisticially significant, suggesting that 'The *Reading* and *Arithmetic* Indexes ... might well be important screening tools for applicants ... if a company wishes to ensure that new employees have the minimum levels of proficiency to cope with the job requirements'. Tables of industrial norms are available for a number of jobs. Combined norms, in the form of percentiles, are provided separately for white and non-white workers, under the headings unskilled, semiskilled, skilled, office and technical.

Using the Test

Instructions on **administration** presuppose some experience of testing; details of the administrator's script are perfectly clear. Examinees require a copy of the test, scrap paper and two pencils. **Scoring** is easy; the scorer tears off the candidate's response sheet and totals the responses made in boxes joined by lines, each of which corresponds to one domain. These can be summed to produce a raw score. The criteria of proficiency requires the candidate to score 80 per cent of the available marks.

Interpretation of results is rather difficult since the normative data supplied are quite inappropriate for UK users (or indeed, anyone). Poor performance on any subtest should give cause for concern, but good performance reveals nothing other than mastery of a narrow range of technical skills. No indication is given as to where and when these skills might be deployed.

Evaluation

The Test sets out to assess a range of technical skills in arithmetic. It has been designed primarily for use in industry, to comply, apparently, with American legislation on fairness in selection (so that job applicants should not be rejected on the basis of measures irrelevant to job performance). Successful use in the world of employment requires detailed job analysis; some suggestions are offered about jobs which require particular arithmetic skills. In the context of UK selection practices, the Test seems designed to solve a problem not encountered in this country.

The Manual is far too deficient in important information to allow the Test to have many sensible uses for educational purposes. Standardizing data, such as it is, could not possibly be used to make normative judgements about schoolchildren in the UK; no data are available concerning ages and attainment. Discussions about 'levels' of performance seem inappropriate, and 'difficulty' might be a more accurate word. No attempt is made to relate criteria of proficiency to descriptions of the tasks that children can actually perform when they have attained these proficiency levels.

THE STAFFORDSHIRE TEST OF COMPUTATION

M.E. Hebron and W. Pattinson
Publication date unspecified;
Standardization date unspecified;
Revised 1974; Manual revised 1974
Harrap, UK
7:00–14:11 (7:00–14:11)
Group
Untimed (no estimate given)
Standard Scores in one-year age bands
Consumable sheets for Sheet 1, reusable question sheets for Sheet 2 (users supply paper)

Item Distribution

	Number	Measurement	Space	Algebra	Logic	Statistics
Comprehension	11	–	–	–	–	–
Technique	73	–	–	–	–	–
Recall	7	–	–	–	–	–

Presentation						
Words	Numbers	Algebra	Figures	Graphs	Pictures	Oral
30	87	–	–	–	–	1

Response			
Free Format	Forced Choice	Constructed Lines	Explanation
91	–	–	–

Context		
Abstract	Concrete	Total
47	44	91

Purposes

'… [It] measures accuracy in computation, sampling comprehensively the skills acquired during the ages seven to 15 years. It implies knowledge of concepts in decimal currency, metric measures and in the more common commercial transactions. It is useful in detecting specific weaknesses in the case of individual pupils, and for establishing a pupil's status within his age group.'

'… [It] can be used as an indication of whether a pupil is working at his true capacity.'

Content

Two sheets are provided. Sheet 1 presents 46 items which involve single– and multiple-digit operations, and operations on decimals. All decimal operations are posed as questions involving money. All the items present number sums; pupils construct responses to each item. Sheet 2 presents 46 items which focus on decimals, fractions, percentages, and ratio. Many of the items are set as word problems, often in semi-realistic contexts such as those involving carpeting, time, interest, exchange rates, piece work, money and the like.

The content is severely dated: 'if there are 2.50 dollars to the pound ...' 'if two men earn £56 in four weeks ...' Several of the tasks require dubious assumptions to be made. For example, 'A machine operator turns out 250 parts per minute. He is paid 0.6 of a penny for every hundred ...' Pupils are asked to calculate a weekly wage, given the number of hours worked per day, and the number of days worked per week. To answer another question, pupils must assume that the Simple Interest formula is relevant in a situation where it is not. Far too many of the problems ask pupils to tackle old-fashioned, stylized problems of a sort which they would, (hopefully), never meet outside this Test.

Test development

No information is given about the choice of test content or about any early trialling. The Test was **standardized** on a total of 4079 pupils in schools in the East Riding and in Norwich, sampled in each school year for pupils aged seven to 14 years. Testing took place in late February, and 450 to 580 pupils were tested in each year group. No details of the year of testing, nor about the sampling procedure, are provided.

Both test scores and score variances increase considerably and rather erratically with age. No details are given about the age standardization method. The Manual presents standard scores for whole year bands. No information is provided about any sex differences which may have emerged.

Split-half **reliability** (based on scores on odd and even numbered items) was 'near unity, ranging from 0.96 ... to 0.97 ...' **Validity** was examined by comparing scores with those obtained on the *Nottingham Number Test* subtests. 'At 9½ years the correlations were 0.86 for Concepts and 0.78 for Skills; at 10 ½ years they were 0.82 and 0.85 respectively.' Sample size was not specified, but high correlations are to be expected, given the similarity of content in the two tests.

Using the Test

Paper and pencils are required. No space is provided on Sheet 2 for pupil answers. Instructions for **administration** are deficient in a number of respects: for example, no suggestion is made that pupils write their names on the script – not that there is any space provided! No general advice about testing practices is offered, and no script is provided for the administrator.

Scoring of Sheet 1 is unremarkable; the Manual is laid out in roughly the same way as the Test, and so can be used as a scoring key. Several items are awarded two marks; no provision is made to guard against marking errors, and no provision is made on the answer sheet to record the raw score.

Scoring of Sheet 2 is made unnecessarily difficult because no pupil response sheets are provided; furthermore, a misprint leads to an error in the allocation of marks for Item 51(b). No internal checks are provided to offset marker errors. No space is allocated for the total score or standardized score to be written.

Derivation of standard scores is straightforward; no discussion about errors of measurement is offered; standard scores can range from 44 to 178, but there is no comment on the unreliability of these extreme scores. The Manual also describes how 'arithmetic age' can be estimated from the table of standard scores. No guidance is offered about the **interpretation** of standard scores; no advice is given about how they can be used.

Evaluation

The purposes of the Test are clearly laid out. In my view, it fails in almost all of its aims. Detailed analysis of the nature of computational skill and the sampling frame for the test items would have helped both the authors and the user. Choice of items is patchy and certainly fails to sample 'comprehensively the skills acquired during the ages 7 to 15 years'. The range of contexts chosen is far too narrow; the items present an excess of technical difficulties, quite irrelevant to the needs of pupils – who are most unlikely to meet elaborate calculations on fractions, or decimals, with no calculator to help them. Too few items require pupils to *select* an appropriate operation. None require estimation or judgements about the reasonableness of answers. 'Realistic' contexts are very dated. No attempt is made by the authors to help users detect 'specific weaknesses in the case of individual pupils ...'. It might, however, be used 'for establishing a pupil's status within his age group' on this rather peculiar mixture of skills. The claim that it 'can be used as an indication of whether a pupil is working at his true capacity' is, at best unproven and, at worst, a doubtful idea altogether.

The Manual is badly printed, and seriously deficient. Details of test administration are inadequate; scoring is difficult and likely to be unreliable. Details of the standardizing sample are inadequate: users are not cautioned about likely errors of measurement, or given any guidance on the interpretation and use of test results.

'Y' MATHEMATICS SERIES : Y1

D. Young
First Published 1979; Standardization
date unspecified
Hodder and Stoughton, UK
7:05–8:10 (7:08–8:08)
Group
Part untimed, part timed; (40 mins)
Standard Scores in one-month age
bands
Consumable booklets

Item Distribution

	Number	Measurement	Space	Algebra	Logic	Statistics
Comprehension	20	–	2	–	1	–
Technique	29	3	2	–	–	–
Recall	–	–	–	–	–	–

Presentation						
Words	Numbers	Algebra	Figures	Graphs	Pictures	Oral
18	41	–	7	1	3	20

Response			
Free Format	Forced Choice	Constructed Lines	Explanation
47	8	–	–

Context		
Abstract	Concrete	Total
26	29	55

Purposes

'... to complement teachers' own assessments. Together with standardized tests of intelligence, reading and spelling, they have provided a framework to which many other observations and opinions have been related, and the records have enabled progress to be followed from year to year throughout the Primary stage. The test results have also helped in making decisions about the referral of pupils and have been used in the initial discussions with educational psychologists, advisers and others concerned with handicapped pupils.'

'Criterion-referenced testing has to be frequent to be effective. By contrast, the Y tests sample a wide variety of skills and topics at relatively long intervals (yearly) and provide, by use of the quotients, a means of relating the results, for individuals or for groups, to other such measures. This is not the aim of detailed testing. Both the larger view and the detailed view are essential: one for general educational guidance and planning, the other for the actual teaching.'

'The Y1 tests mathematical understanding over a wide range of concepts and situations, recognises the importance of language in mathematics and gives due attention to the essential role of computation.'

'The testing of an understanding of number and accuracy in computation has been a prime consideration.'

'The aim has often been to test a topic at the stage where understanding is being developed rather than at a later, more formalised level.'

'can be used, together with the author's *Group Mathematics Test (GMT)* to test groups of various ages and levels of ability .. the equal standards of the tests ... permit ... a firmer evaluation than ... is ... possible using tests drawn from a variety of sources.'

Content

Y1 consists of three parts. The oral section comprises 20 questions on a very wide range of topics, including: ordering; counting; place value; use of basic mathematical operations; reading a bar chart; telling the time; proportions; and logic problems. The computational section consists of 20 written items which involve whole number addition, subtraction, and multiplication. The written problem section presents 20 word problems which require pupils to understand and solve problems set in a number of familiar contexts.

'There have been a number of previous standardized versions of the Y1, each in turn providing a basis for projecting the norms of its slightly modified successor.'

'... teachers' comments have helped to determine the present content.'

'All the items have passed through at least two analyses to establish discriminating power and facility levels.'

The parallel forms are almost identical; item analyses, and other studies confirmed their equivalence.

Standardization was based on the scores of pupils in 'a group of 12 schools known, collectively, to be representative of the national pattern of general ability and achievement because of their records on [unspecified] NFER and Moray House Tests'.

Norms in the Manual are based on a sample of 1209 pupils; no data on sex differences are discussed, and a single set of norms is presented. The date of standardization is not given.

Each Manual in the Y series presents information about performance on tests Y1, Y2, Y3 and Y4 for pupils of different ages. Pupils' performance in two successive years was assessed in one junior school, chosen at random. Group size varied from 51 to 77. Results showed 'a similar level of achievement throughout the school and good agreement between the two medians for the year-groups'.

The user is provided with a table of scores obtained by eight year olds, at five levels of ability, with subscales on each of the oral, computation and written problems: this is based on 250 papers from 77 schools. The Manual also describes the distinguishing characteristics of pupils whose mathematical attainment is being underestimated because of their poor reading ability.

Reliability was assessed by correlating scores on parallel forms of the test, for small numbers of pupils. Correlations ranged from 0.90 to 0.96, corresponding to SEM between 2.0 and 3.0. 'The two forms can be taken to be of equal reliability with a standard error of measurement of 2.5'. The Manual explains how this value can be interpreted in terms of *raw* score.

Construct **validity** was assessed by comparing test scores from 109 pupils aged 7:10½ with those of the *Graded Arithmetic-Mathematics Test*; the resulting correlation was 0.87. This high value is hardly surprising, given the focus on multiple-digit operations also found in the 'validating' test.

One study reported in the Manual would have allowed the calculation of correlations between tests in the Y series; none are reported.

'Another approach to validity is for the user to examine the content of the test. The overlap with his own programme need not be complete to ensure satisfactory validity since ... the general factor that runs through the test items would almost certainly be found in other possible inclusions.'

Using the Test

Pencils are required; erasers are not to be provided. Instructions for **administration** are sensible and clear; the Manual recommends that adjacent pupils be given alternative forms of the Test. Part of the Test is administered orally; the remainder is timed. Instructions for **scoring** are clear. The Manual contains a list of answers for both forms of the Test. A scoring key would facilitate marking, however, and some internal checks against scorer error would be useful. Three subscores are produced. These are added, and used to refer the user to a standard score (called a 'quotient'). No reliability estimates are offered for the subscores; the SEM is not incorporated into the score.

For score **interpretation**, the Manual recommends that teachers should compare the rank order of pupils' raw scores with their own judgements. Discrepancies of more than 10 points between the standard scores on these tests and on tests of reading and intelligence, should be investigated. (The first stage of the investigation should be to check scoring, and to look for pupil errors such as failing to notice a column of computations.) If these checks fail to account for differences, the parallel form of the Test can be given. If differences are still apparent, 'the only responsible attitude is an active, hopeful, one' in an attempt to remediate deficiencies. (The

Manual points out that it cannot be assumed that all differences *are* remediable.)

> 'Comparisons of group performances in the oral, computation and written problem sections can of course be made if this appears likely to throw light on the relative strengths and weaknesses of the present teaching programme.'

Evaluation

This Test is one of a series which covers the junior age range. The Manual takes time to explain the purposes for which the Test was developed, and the way that results can be used. Details of administration and scoring are sensible and clear, although scoring would be appreciably easier were a scoring key provided, together with some checks against marker errors.

Test content is rather narrow, and focuses heavily on basic mathematical operations.

> 'Potential users will no doubt ... regret omissions. This should not ... be a matter for fundamental concern. The items within tests can vary without altering the large common factor that runs through them, and success with one set of items is predictable from performance on another set even when there are superficially wide differences.'

I have no sympathy with this view. The content of a test *is* a matter for fundamental concern. Assessment should be linked to education; it is not a goal in itself.

The Manual is deficient in many technical respects: too little information is given about the samples used (even the standardization date is omitted), many of them are small, and too little attention is paid to SEM.

'Y' MATHEMATICS SERIES : Y2

D. Young
First Published 1979; Standardization
date unspecified
Hodder and Stoughton, UK
F Table 8:05–9:10 (8:08–9:08)
X Table for poor readers and slow
learners 8:05–14:10 (11:00–14:08)
Group
Part untimed, part timed; (35 mins)
Standard Scores in one-month age
bands
Consumable booklets

Item Distribution

	Number	Measurement	Space	Algebra	Logic	Statistics
Comprehension	20	2	2	1	1	–
Technique	28	4	–	–	–	–
Recall	–	–	–	–	–	–

Presentation						
Words	Numbers	Algebra	Figures	Graphs	Pictures	Oral
15	51	1	9	2	3	20

Response			
Free Format	Forced Choice	Constructed Lines	Explanation
50	5	–	–

Context		
Abstract	Concrete	Total
26	29	55

Purposes

'The test was designed to be suitable for a wide range of pupils
upwards from second-year Juniors to older backward pupils in the
secondary stage.'
    See also *Purposes* in the review of Y1.

Content

The structure of the Test is the same as that of Y1, and consists of
an untimed oral section, and a timed section which presents

20 multiple-digit operations in numeric form, followed by 15 word problems. Two versions of the Test can be given; one aimed at Juniors, and one aimed at low-attaining secondary school children. The latter do not face the word problems. Overall, the test focuses on the use of basic number operations, together with items on fractions, ratio and proportion, counting, number series, using graphs and tables, and telling the time.

Test development

See *Test development* in the review of Y1.

'The selection of items was guided by analysis of the responses of both second-year Juniors and backward secondary pupils.'

As in the case of test Y1, two item analyses are mentioned, as is a description of pupils in a group of 12 schools known, collectively, to be representative of the national pattern of general ability and achievement because of their records on (unspecified) NFER and Moray House Tests. 'The scores of the secondary pupils (in six schools) were directly calibrated from such test results.'

Two tables of norms are provided: the F table provides standard scores for Juniors; the X table provides standard scores for less able secondary school children, and is based on the first 40 items of Y2 only.

1269 pupils aged 8:08 to 9:08 took part in the **standardization** of the F table. This sample was also used in the standardization of the X table, along with a sample of 1169 pupils aged 11:00 to 14:08. Values given for the X table between 9:08 and 11:00 are interpolated; some evidence about the accuracy of the interpolation is offered, based on a sample of 140 pupils who took Y3, then Y4 and Y2 eight months later. Values for pupils aged 8:05 to 8:07 are extrapolated.

> 'Since some of the secondary groups could be expected to contain a high proportion of pupils with a reading age of less than eight years ... a test normed independently of reading age was required ... a test of forty items, as in the first two sections, was sufficient for adequate discrimination between the backward secondary pupils.'

A table of scores obtained by nine year olds at five levels of ability on each of the oral, computation and written problems subscales is provided, based on 250 papers from 74 schools.

Reliability was assessed for six groups of pupils (219 in all) aged 9:03 by comparing performance on forms A and B tested two to three weeks apart. Reliability coefficients varied from 0.88 to 0.93, corresponding to between 2.4 and 3.0 points of raw score. 'The two forms can be taken to be of equal reliability with a standard error of measurement 2.8.'

Construct **validity** was assessed by comparing test scores with those obtained on the *Graded Arithmetic–Mathematics Test*; for a sample of 152 pupils aged 8:11, correlation between raw scores was 0.88. This value is not surprising, given that both tests focus on such basic mathematical operations. Correlations with other tests are offered for Y2 X scores of 130 pupils aged 11:06 with reading ages less than 9:05, as follows: *SPAR Reading*, 0.39; *SPAR Spelling*, 0.37; *Oral Verbal Intelligence Test*, 0.56. For a further sample of 131 pupils aged 14:02½, correlations with Y2 X scores were: *SPAR Reading*, 0.24; *SPAR Spelling*, 0.01; *Oral Verbal Intelligence Test*, 0.59; *NFER Non-Verbal Test DH*, 0.63. We can conclude that Y2 X score does not depend heavily on reading skills.

'Another approach to validity is for the user to examine the content of the test. The overlap with his own programme need not be complete to ensure satisfactory validity since ... the general factor that runs through the test items would almost certainly be found in other possible inclusions.'

Using the Test

See *Using the Test* in the review of Y1. Pupils require pencils and rulers marked in centimetres and millimetres; erasers should not be provided. Details for **administration** and **scoring** are clear; a key would facilitate marking. For the **interpretation** of scores, similar advice to that provided in Y1 is offered.

In addition, for 'Backward junior and secondary pupils ... The examination of the results should begin with comparisons with the teacher's opinions and other information on the pupils' record cards.'

'At the secondary stage ... agreement between the mathematics quotients and those for intelligence, reading and spelling is less than in the primary school, but the recognition and confirmation of unusual patterns of ability may still be of importance for remedial or guidance purposes.'

'The only pupils whose mathematics scores might be seriously affected are those of high mathematical ability with less than average reading ability. The table of X quotients can be used ... It would ... be a misuse of this table to refer to it for pupils whose reading was demonstrably adequate but whose ability to deal with written problems was nevertheless poor.'

Evaluation

See *Evaluation* in the review of Y1. This Test is one of a series which covers the junior age range. Purposes, details of administration and scoring are presented clearly. The spread of content is less narrow than on Y1, but the focus of the Test is still predominantly basic mathematical operations. The author has taken a rather cavalier approach to content validity. This is particularly the case in the use of the X scale. This scale is intended for use with secondary pupils who have reading difficulties. It seems somewhat perverse to simply remove word problems from the assessment of their mathematical attainment, because they have difficulty reading them. It would be preferable to extend the oral section to cover more complex problems, even at the cost of lengthier and more difficult administration.

The Manual suffers the same deficiencies as Y1, in terms of the absence of information about pupil samples, and the lack of attention paid to SEM.

'Y' MATHEMATICS SERIES : Y3 and Y4

D. Young
First Published 1979; Standardization
date unspecified
Hodder and Stoughton, UK
Y3 9:05–10:10 (Standardization age
range unclear)
Y4 10:05–11:10 (Standardization age
range unclear)
Group
Timed; 30 mins
Standard Scores in one-month age
bands
Consumable booklets

TEST Y3
Item Distribution

	Number	Measurement	Space	Algebra	Logic	Statistics
Comprehension	9	1	1	–	1	1
Technique	22	9	2	–	–	–
Recall	3	–	–	–	–	–

Presentation						
Words	Numbers	Algebra	Figures	Graphs	Pictures	Oral
30	40	–	8	5	–	–

Response			
Free Format	Forced Choice	Constructed Lines	Explanation
50	–	–	–

Context		
Abstract	Concrete	Total
26	24	50

TEST Y4
Item Distribution

	Number	Measurement	Space	Algebra	Logic	Statistics
Comprehension	10	5	4	–	3	–
Technique	22	4	1	–	–	–
Recall	1	–	2	–	–	–

Presentation						
Words	Numbers	Algebra	Figures	Graphs	Pictures	Oral
30	47	1	10	5	–	–

Response			
Free Format	Forced Choice	Constructed Lines	Explanation
50	–	–	–

Context		
Abstract	Concrete	Total
24	26	50

Purposes

See *Purposes* in the review of Y1.

Content

Neither Y3 nor Y4 have an oral section. Both consist of 20 items devoted to computational skill, presented in numeric form; and 30 items assessing a range of skills, in written form. Overall, Y3 and Y4 assess basic number operations on multiple digits, decimals, fractions, ratio and proportion, reading data presented graphically, calculation of perimeters and areas, use of co-ordinates, and calculations involving time.

Written items are attractively presented and interesting, especially when compared to items in earlier Y-series tests. Unlike Y1 and Y2, no parallel forms are available.

Test development

See *Test development* in the review of Y1.

'There have been a number of previous standardized versions of
the Y3 and Y4, each in turn providing a basis for projecting the
norms of its slightly modified successor.'

Standardization is described as follows: 'The questions are
derived from "banks" formed from the material used in a series
of tests provided for use in schools over a period of more than
ten years. The series of analyses ... enabled discriminating
power to be established and the accuracy of facility levels to be
progressively improved.'

'The standardization here is based on the scores of pupils in a
group of 12 schools known, collectively, to be representative of
the national pattern of general ability and achievement because
of their records on [unspecified] NFER and Moray House Tests.'

Standard scores are presented on Y3 for pupils aged 9:05 to 10:10
based on a sample of 1285; the age range for Y4 is 10:05 to 11:10
based on a sample of 1267. No information is given about the age
range of the pupils within these samples; no information is given
about sex differences, or even about the date of testing.

A single table, showing mean scores on word problems and
computation at five different ability levels, is based on 250 papers
for each of Y3 (pupils aged 10 years) and Y4 (pupils aged 11 years)
obtained from 72 schools. This can be used to ascertain whether 'a
pupil's conceptual development is not keeping pace with his
conceptual skills.' It can also be used to identify children whose
mathematical attainment may be being underassessed because of
reading difficulties.

Reliability was estimated via KR–20, using 637 Y3 papers and
657 Y4 papers (pupil ages unspecified); values obtained of 0.96
and 0.97 respectively correspond to SEM of 2.2 and 2.1 on raw
scores.

To examine concurrent **validity** 'The Y3 and Y4 were correlated
with the *Graded Arithmetic-Mathematics Test* ... and the coefficients were respectively 0.88 ... and 0.94 ...' These are

correlations between raw scores. The age range of pupils, and sample sizes are not stated.

Using the Test

See *Using the Test* in the review of Y1. Pupils require pencils; erasers and rulers should not be provided. Details for **administration** and **scoring** are clear; a key would facilitate scoring.

For the **interpretation** of scores, similar advice to that provided in Y1 is offered. The answers for Y4 contain errors, unlike those for Y1, Y2 and Y3. Printing errors have led to rainfall being measured in 'min' (not 'mm'), and dogs are counted in 'days' (not 'dogs'). The answer to Question 5 is wrong.

Evaluation

See *Evaluation* in the review of Y1. These tests form part of a series which covers the junior age range. Purposes, details of administration and scoring are presented clearly. The spread of content widens as tests are intended for use with older children, although multiple-digit operations presented in numerical form still figure large.

All the Manuals are seriously deficient in the information they provide about pupil samples, reliability and SEM.

YARDSTICKS: CRITERION-REFERENCED TESTS IN MATHEMATICS

National Foundation for Educational Research
First Published 1975 (adapted from USA tests); Unstandardized; Reprinted with corrections 1977, 1978, 1979, 1980
NFER-NELSON, UK
The first six years of school (not standardized)
Group
Untimed
Raw Scores; Criterion referenced; diagnostic
Consumable booklets

LEVEL I

Item Distribution

	Number	Measurement	Space	Algebra	Logic	Statistics
Comprehension	3	–	–	–	2	–
Technique	157	5	1	–	–	–
Recall	21	–	4	–	–	–

Presentation						
Words	Numbers	Algebra	Figures	Graphs	Pictures	Oral
190	186	–	36	–	–	190

Response			
Free Format	Forced Choice	Constructed Lines	Explanation
–	190	–	–

Context		
Abstract	Concrete	Total
155	35	190

LEVEL 2
Item Distribution

	Number	Measurement	Space	Algebra	Logic	Statistics
Comprehension	16	–	–	–	–	–
Technique	132	5	5	–	5	–
Recall	27	–	15	–	–	–

Presentation

Words	Numbers	Algebra	Figures	Graphs	Pictures	Oral
200	185	–	45	–	1	–

Response

Free Format	Forced Choice	Constructed Lines	Explanation
–	200	–	–

Context

Abstract	Concrete	Total
144	56	200

LEVEL 3
Item Distribution

	Number	Measurement	Space	Algebra	Logic	Statistics
Comprehension	27	1	–	–	6	–
Technique	168	19	20	–	–	–
Recall	26	–	15	–	–	–

Presentation

Words	Numbers	Algebra	Figures	Graphs	Pictures	Oral
245	230	–	52	5	–	–

Response

Free Format	Forced Choice	Constructed Lines	Explanation
–	245	–	–

Context

Abstract	Concrete	Total
167	78	245

LEVEL 4
Item Distribution

	Number	Measurement	Space	Algebra	Logic	Statistics
Comprehension	88	1	6	–	19	–
Technique	411	44	54	–	–	–
Recall	11	–	28	–	–	–

Presentation

Words	Numbers	Algebra	Figures	Graphs	Pictures	Oral
510	480	6	98	10	1	–

Response

Free Format	Forced Choice	Constructed Lines	Explanation
–	510	–	–

Context

Abstract	Concrete	Total
340	170	510

LEVEL 5
Item Distribution

	Number	Measurement	Space	Algebra	Logic	Statistics
Comprehension	80	–	28	–	–	–
Technique	372	50	65	–	50	10
Recall	–	–	30	–	–	–

Presentation

Words	Numbers	Algebra	Figures	Graphs	Pictures	Oral
540	494	10	124	10	–	–

Response

Free Format	Forced Choice	Constructed Lines	Explanation
–	540	–	–

Context

Abstract	Concrete	Total
359	181	540

<small>LEVEL</small> 6
Item Distribution

	Number	Measurement	Space	Algebra	Logic	Statistics
Comprehension	111	5	37	8	16	15
Technique	347	5	29	–	4	5
Recall	15	–	7	–	10	–

Presentation						
Words	Numbers	Algebra	Figures	Graphs	Pictures	Oral
560	533	62	62	20	–	–

Response			
Free Format	Forced Choice	Constructed Lines	Explanation
–	560	–	–

Context		
Abstract	Concrete	Total
414	146	560

Purposes

'A criterion-referenced test – comparing the behavioural objectives with the sets of questions that test the child's grasp of each objective.'

'The tests identify the stages of growth in mathematics. The stages are enumerated in terms of behavioural objectives, and for each objective there is a group of test questions. After the children have worked on a particular skills area in class … the teacher can follow up immediately with the corresponding set … of questions to discover whether mastery has taken place.'

'… to provide teachers with a means of monitoring their pupils' individual progress in mathematics.'

'… it is possible to identify:

a) weaknesses of the class as a whole, or groups within it,
b) individuals who are weak in particular areas,
c) individuals who are generally weak and may require special attention.'

Content

Yardsticks consist of 2245 test items presented in six pupil booklets, each one corresponding to a different level of work aimed at the first six years of schooling. The series identifies 657 behavioural objectives in mathematics; each booklet presents groups of items to test if each objective has been met. In Levels 1 to 3, five items are used to assess each criterion; in Levels 4 to 6, 10 items assess each one.

Level 1 presents items whose objectives are classified under number, addition and subtraction, equations and inequalities, applied arithmetic, and geometry. In Level 2, headings are number, addition and subtraction, multiplication and division, equations and inequalities, sets, applied arithmetic, fractions, and geometry. In Level 3, headings are addition and subtraction, multiplication and division, sets, applied arithmetic, fractions, and geometry. In Levels 4, 5 and 6, headings are number, addition and subtraction, multiplication and division, equations and inequalities, sets, applied arithmetic, fractions, decimals, and geometry.

All the items involve words, and technical mathematical language abounds, together with occasional anachronistic phrases such as 'what numeral names the sum?' (which means 'work out').

Test development

It is clear from the list of objectives that a good deal of thought has gone into the development of *Yardsticks*. A serious deficiency of the Manual is that no attempt is made to explain the rationale which must underlie the list of objectives, or to describe early development work. Instead, users are told that the scheme of tests was first developed in the USA (where it was published in 1973), 'following extensive research into many programmes for teaching mathematics during the first six years of schooling'. Topics were grouped according to difficulty, and a number of different authors wrote items, each of which was then 'checked for consistency and validity in measuring its particular objective'. Before publication in the UK,

> 'the entire programme was carefully evaluated by a panel of British educationalists. Many objectives were rewritten or replaced, and the test questions were examined and reconstructed or rewritten where necessary to conform with UK courses and practices. Practising teachers were involved from the outset, both to assess the content of the tests and to try them out in their schools. As a result, both the behavioural objectives and the test content are entirely appropriate to British education.'

This description is, at best, almost useless, and at worst, patronizing. The authors assert that 'children ... learn through a progression of stages, achieving mastery at each before they proceed to the next. It is this progressive consideration that is so crucial in mathematics.' Also, 'Mastery must be achieved before children can move on to more complex learning situations; and if mastery has not taken place, then the teacher must work with the children concerned to achieve it.' Consequently, 'The behavioural objectives are structured according to a gradually increasing level of difficulty'.

No justification is offered for the balance of contents. No attempt is made to explain the structure of the behavioural objectives. No evidence is produced to suggest that implicit theories have any grounding in reality. No evidence is offered to support assertions about the distinction between different levels, or the reality of groupings of different objectives. Since the Test is criterion-referenced, no attempt is made to offer normative scores of any kind. No evidence relates to **reliability** or to **validity**; there are no descriptions of how *Yardsticks* has been used.

Using the Test

Three uses are suggested. First, to assess pupil mastery immediately after a topic has been covered in class: brief but frequent testing is recommended so that pupil difficulties can be dealt with quickly. Secondly, to test a completed sequence of work by presenting pupils with a test composed of items which assess appropriately grouped objectives. Thirdly, by grouping a large collection of items together (reflecting a large number of objectives) revision tests can be constructed which might indicate areas of particular difficulty, in need of further work.

The Manual suggests that the diagnostic aspects of testing should be emphasized to pupils before test **administration**. Pupils require a pencil, eraser and scrap paper. A model script is provided, to introduce pupils to the test format, which users are invited to amend. Detailed instructions, to be given verbatim, are provided for assessing each mathematical procedure. These are clear and sensible.

Each pupil booklet contains sample questions, the test questions, and histograms which pupils complete to record their progress on each behavioural objective. These histograms describe the processes to be mastered, provide space for pupils to record total scores and to present these data graphically, and leave space for teacher comments.

Associated with each pupil booklet is a management guide which provides a description of the test scheme, instructions for test administration, lists of the behavioural objectives sampled at this level and for the whole series, and a class record. In addition, an answer book is available for each pupil booklet, presented in an identical format. Unfortunately, at the time of reviewing, answer booklets were not available; no comment can be made about their accuracy, or their ease of use for **scoring**. Pupils can be encouraged to record their own progress, and presumably can also mark each other's work, to avoid an undue clerical load on the teacher.

The **interpretation** of scores is direct; pupils who fail to answer correctly all the items under a particular behavioural objective should receive further instruction and practice until they *can* master them. Failure to attain mastery at lower levels is likely to have dire consequences when later levels are attempted. No suggestions are made about the kinds of remediation which might improve performance on different objectives.

Evaluation

Yardsticks provides an extensive resource pool of items, grouped together so as to assess similar behavioural objectives. These objectives are stated clearly. Since pupils record their own progress, and have access to the descriptions of the items, these descriptions may well provide a useful vehicle for discussing progress with individuals at a level which they can do something about, rather than merely being exhorted to 'try harder'. The analysis of mathematics problems at this micro level may well have a useful in-service training function, too, since it encourages everyone to reflect on sources of difficulty, and likely pupil misconceptions.

Nevertheless, the scheme has a number of major deficiencies. Since it offers a logically based, 'bottom-up' view of mathematical skills, pupils must be technically proficient in arithmetic before they handle 'applied' problems (such as giving change, calculating volumes, sharing sweets and the like). Few educators (or mathematicians) would look favourably on this view; if pupils are to be encouraged to achieve 'mastery', they need to see some benefits from the formalisms they are offered, and mathematical systems must be seen to be helpful in real situations. Mathematics *has* no simple structure; trying to offer one is unlikely to have a desirable effect in class. Early levels focus very heavily on assessing technical skills, later ones involve a good deal of comprehension: all levels lack focus on conceptual issues.

An increased emphasis on mastery learning and the eradication of error is welcome. Nevertheless, the notion that pupils must master *every* aspect of each topic they encounter is hard to justify, and if followed slavishly might lead to some awful educational experiences for pupils.

The Manual fails to justify the choice of objectives, or the choice of items. Without this justification, and supporting evidence, *Yardsticks* can hardly claim to be an advance on any other set of books offering a collection of related items on small tests.

It is hard to see how *Yardsticks* might be used. Pupils at any age would probably require books at several levels to fully assess their attainment (given the wide spread in attainment by pupils of different ages), thereby increasing the cost of use, and the awkwardness of administration. The booklets themselves could not be used as the basis for a course of mathematics.

Finally, the language used in the Management Guide is somewhat strange; readers are cajoled and directed rather than informed in a neutral way. Nouns magically transmute into verbs, rhetoric abounds, and absolute certainty is seeded with doubt. For example:

'What then is mastery ...? Mastery denotes total success, and it is total success we are seeking. So ultimate mastery of a mathematics objective is the ability to answer all the questions correctly. Perhaps one error is tolerable. Two errors suggests all is not well ...'

In its present form, *Yardsticks* is not to be recommended. It offers promise of a useful set of assessment aids which, unfortunately it cannot fulfil.

Appendix 1
References

COCKCROFT, W.H. (1982). *Mathematics Counts*. London: HMSO.

LEVY, P., and GOLDSTEIN, H. (1984). *Tests in Education*.   London: Academic Press.

RIDGWAY, J. (1988). *Assessing Mathematical Attainment*. Windsor: NFER-NELSON.

Appendix 2
Glossary

age standardization: the purpose of age standardization is to allow children of a particular age to be judged with respect to children of the same age as themselves, rather than with children who are either older or younger.

blueprint: is a specification of the content of a test, and the processes assessed.

confidence interval: is the general form of which a *score band* is a particular example. All statistics (means, standard deviations, etc.) can have confidence intervals calculated for them, when they are estimated.

correlation: correlation coefficient: a measure of the association between two sets of scores. It can be calculated in different ways, depending on the statistical assumptions made. Values lie between +1.00 (perfect association) and −1.00 (perfect disassociation). A value of 0.00 shows that two sets of scores are completely unrelated. All correlation coefficients quoted in this volume are Pearson product-moment correlations unless otherwise stated.

criterion referencing: see page 4.

decile: a score has a decile rank of d if *d* x 10 per cent of scores fall at or below that score.

diagnostic test: see page 4.

equivalent forms: see parallel tests.

factor analysis: is a collection of statistical techniques which attempt to uncover the underlying structure of a set of variables (for example tests, or test items). The procedures assume that the inter-relationships between things which have been observed can be accounted for by a small number of underlying variables or dimensions or 'factors'. Factor analysis is an attempt to determine these underlying factors and to account for each variable in terms of a combination of factors.

Guttman's Scalogram Analysis: a statistical package for the analysis of tests thought to form *hierarchies*.

hierarchy: is a set of tests where success at higher levels depends on success at lower levels.

homogeneity: items are said to be homogeneous when they all appear to be measuring the same thing: tests are said to be homogeneous when they have a high degree of internal reliability.

item: is the basic unit of a test – for example, a single question. Any aspect of the test for which a score is derived is considered to be an item – so individual questions might consist of multiple items (although this is rather uncommon).

item analysis: when test constructors set out to design tests, it is common for them to try out a large number of items. Exploratory studies allow test constructors to investigate the difficulty of particular items; the inter-relationship between items; the way items discriminate between different children at different ages, and other statistical properties of the items. This range of procedures is called item analysis.

item discrimination: a whole test will identify high– and low-attaining pupils. Item discrimination refers to the extent to which an individual item will distinguish between high and low attainers.

item difficulty: the proportion of pupils who fail to answer an item correctly.

item facility: the proportion of pupils who answer an item correctly.

KR–20, KR–21 (Kuder-Richardson formulae 20 and 21): these are methods for calculating the *internal consistency* of a test.

levels of understanding: pupils' understanding of particular topic areas sometimes appears to undergo qualitative shifts. Different states or stages can be described as levels of understanding.

Loevinger's H: some tests set out to identify qualitatively different levels of understanding or skill. On any item which illustrates a high level of understanding, there should be few pupils who answer this item successfully, having failed an item at a lower level. *H* is a measure of the extent to which an item satisfies this expectation.

mathematical age: see *mental age.*

mean: the arithmetic average of a set of scores.

mental age: during standardization, average scores can be calculated for pupils in each age group sampled. These scores can then be taken to define 'mental ages'. The terminology is quite misleading. It would be wrong to suggest, for example, that a low-attaining 14-year-old is functioning like an average eight-year-old.

normal score distribution: is any distribution of scores which follows the normal or Gaussian distribution.

norms, norm referencing, normative: see page 4.

number age: see mental age.

parallel tests, or parallel forms: are tests which have been designed to be equivalent in terms of what they measure and the scores they produce. Parallel tests are also designed to have identical statistical characteristics and to be strongly correlated with each other.

percentile, percentile rank: a score has a percentile rank of *p* if *p* per cent of scores fall at or below that score.

phi coefficient: is a *correlation coefficient* used when both variables to be correlated are dichotomous, for example sex, and examination pass or failure.

practice test: any preliminary test which is intended to familiarize pupils with the test format, the test situation and the like. Practice tests are not scored.

profile: tests which provide scores for an individual on a number of subtests provide *profiles* of each candidate. These are often displayed graphically with reference to normal score distributions obtained on each subtest to offer the test user a pattern of peaks and troughs which represent the relative strengths and weaknesses of each pupil.

raw score: is the number of questions answered correctly, or the time taken to perform a test or some combination of correct responses and incorrect responses, etc. A raw score on its own has little significance.

reliability: see page 14.

sampling: in order to present test norms, a large collection of pupils must be tested. These pupils, hopefully, will be representative of the school population for whom the test is intended. The process of choosing these pupils is called *sampling*. Several different sampling methods exist.

score band: all measurements are prone to error. Reporting a pupil's attainment as a single score can hide this fact, and can lead to the over interpretation of small differences between scores. Scores should be reported as score bands, which incorporate an estimate of the probability that the pupil's score lies within the given band.

SD: see *standard deviation*.

SEM: see *standard error of measurement*.

Spearman's rho: is a *correlation coefficient* calculated in a way that does not make strong statistical assumptions about the distribution of the two sets of scores.

standard deviation (SD): when pupils are tested, a range of scores is obtained. The standard deviation is a measure of the degree of spread of scores. If scores conform to a normal distribution, the SD and the mean provide a succinct summary of the distribution, and the score from any individual can easily be related to the scores of the whole population. For example, 68 per cent of a large sample of scores lie within one standard deviation of the mean; about 95 per cent of scores lie within two standard deviations; and about 99 per cent of scores lie within three standard deviations of the mean.

standard error of measurement (SEM): every measure is likely to contain error. A pupil's score on a test is an estimate of their 'true score'; the SEM offers a measure of how accurate this estimate is likely to be. It can be used to construct *score bands* of known accuracy; for example one can be 95 per cent certain that, for a pupil of average ability, their true score lies in the range: test score ±2 SEM.

standard score; standard age score: a scoring scheme where the mean score in each age group is set to 100, and the standard deviation to 15. Standard scores are commonly used because they are easily interpreted (for instance pupils of different ages who have the same standard score can be judged to be performing equally well with respect to their peers), and because they have useful statistical properties, notably than an estimate of the accuracy of measurement can be incorporated into the score relatively easily.

stanine: a 'standard nine' score scale which ranges from 1 to 9 with a mean of 5, and a standard deviation of 2.

target population: the individuals with whom the test is designed to be used; for example, children aged 11:00 to 12:00 in British schools.

test: a collection of items which are administered and scored together, having been developed into a coherent whole in the eyes of the constructor. Tests may be made up of 'subtests' which are groups of items which are separately evaluated.

validity: see page 14.

variance: a measure of the degree of spread of scores: it is the square of the standard deviation.

Appendix 3
Publisher Index

Harrap Limited, 19–23 Ludgate Hill, London EC4M 7PD
Hodder and Stoughton Educational, PO Box 702, Dunton Green, Sevenoaks, Kent TN13 2YD
The NFER-NELSON Publishing Company Limited, Darville House, 2 Oxford Road East, Windsor, Berkshire SL4 1DF
Science Research Associates Limited, Newtown Road, Henley-on-Thames, Oxfordshire RG9 1EW
The Test Agency Limited, Cournswood House, North Dean, High Wycombe, Bucks HP14 4NW.

Appendix 4
Summary Table

Name	Age Range	Number	Measurement	Space	Algebra	Logic	Statistics	Recall	Technique	Comprehension	Abstract	Concrete	Total Items	Administration	Time (untimed)	Form of Scores	Latest Revision	Specimen	Each Test	Page
				Domain				Process			Context							Cost		
Basic Number Diagnostic Test:	5:00–7:00	50	–	–	–	–	–	10	40	–	20	30	50	I,O	(25)	C,D,M,F	1980	C	C	45
Yardsticks:																				
Level 1	5:00–11:00	181	5	5	–	2	–	25	163	5	155	35	190	G	(–)	C,D	1975	M	E	179
Level 2	5:00–11:00	175	5	20	–	5	–	42	147	16	144	56	200	G	(–)	C,D	1975	M	E	180
Level 3	5:00–11:00	221	20	35	–	6	–	41	207	34	167	78	245	G	(–)	C,D	1975	M	E	180
Level 4	5:00–11:00	510	45	88	–	19	–	39	509	114	340	170	510	G	(–)	C,D	1975	M	E	181
Level 5	5:00–11:00	452	50	123	–	50	10	30	547	108	359	181	540	G	(–)	C,D	1975	M	E	181
Level 6	5:00–11:00	473	10	73	8	30	20	32	390	192	414	146	560	G	(–)	C,D	1975	M	E	182
Graded Arithmetic – **Junior**	5:03–11:08	56	3	3	7	2	1	9	45	18	50	20	70	G	30	S,M	1976	C	C	87
Mathematics Test: **Senior**	11:06–19:00	37	2	14	17	2	3	9	41	25	39	26	65	G	30	S,M	1976	C	C	88

Name	Age Range	Content — Domain: Number	Measurement	Space	Algebra	Logic	Statistics	Content — Process: Recall	Technique	Comprehension	Context: Abstract	Concrete	Total Items	Administration	Time (untimed)	Form of Scores	Latest Revision	Cost: Specimen	Each Test	Page
Group Mathematics Test (See also Y1–Y4)	6:05–12:10	49	3	4	–	6	–	–	33	29	34	24	58	G	(50)	P	1970	C	C	93
Basic Mathematics: Test A	6:09–8:06	22	12	9	–	1	–	1	17	26	10	30	40	G,O	(45)	S.D	1971	C	M	24
Test B	8:04–9:10	21	13	11	–	7	–	–	9	43	12	28	40	G,O	(45)	S.D	1971	C	M	29
Test C	9:07–10:10	32	6	10	2	13	–	–	26	37	22	28	50	G	(50)	S.D	1970	C	M	33
Test DE	10:05–11:11	23	12	9	6	14	2	–	15	51	28	27	55	G	(50)	S.D	1969	C	M	37
Test FG	12:00–15:00	35	12	10	8	12	3	3	12	65	39	16	55	G,O	(–)	S	1969	C	M	41
Basic Number Screening Test	7:00–12:00	32	–	–	–	1	–	2	20	9	24	6	30	G,O	(35)	M	1976	C	C	50
Mathematics Attainment: Test A	7:00–8:06	31	7	12	–	3	–	3	13	35	16	26	42	G,O	(45)	S	1970	C	M	115
Test B	8:06–10:06	30	6	11	1	8	–	5	11	40	16	26	42	G	(45)	S	1970	C	M	119
Test C1	9:00–12:00	36	12	6	2	7	–	2	21	40	13	37	50	G	(50)	S	1970	C	M	122
Test DE2	10:00–11:11	23	8	8	4	12	2	3	12	40	24	22	46	G	(50)	S	1970	C	M	125
Test EF	11:00–13:06	30	8	18	4	3	3	17	27	22	22	38	60	G	(50)	S	1972	M	C	128
The Staffordshire Test of Computation	7:00–14:11	91	–	–	–	–	–	7	73	11	47	44	91	G	(–)	S	1974	O	O	162
'Y' Mathematics Series: (See also Group Mathematics Test) Y1	7:05–8:10	49	3	4	–	1	–	–	34	23	26	29	55	G	(40)	S	1979	C	C	166
Y2	8:05–14:08	48	6	2	1	1	–	–	32	26	26	29	55	G	(35)	S	1979	C	C	171
Y3	9:05–10:10	34	10	3	–	1	2	3	34	13	26	24	50	G	30	S	1979	C	C	175
Y4	10:05–11:10	33	9	7	–	3	–	3	27	22	24	26	50	G	30	S	1979	C	C	176

Leicester Number Test (See also Nottingham Number Test)	7:01–9:00	72	–	2	–	10	–	1	51	32	47	27	74	G.O	(50)	S.P	1970	C	M	99
Mathematics 8 to 12:																				
8	7:06–8:11	27	10	4	–	1	–	5	16	21	17	19	36	G,O	(45)	S,P,D	1984	C	C	103
9	8:06–9:11	32	12	10	–	1	–	8	27	20	19	31	50	G	(45)	S,P,D	1983	C	C	104
10	9:06–10:11	28	13	14	1	2	–	6	21	31	17	33	50	G	(45)	S,P,D	1983	C	C	104
11	10:06–11:11	29	13	12	–	1	–	8	24	23	15	35	50	G	(45)	S,P,D	1983	C	C	105
12	11:06–12:11	29	14	6	1	3	–	4	22	27	20	30	50	G	(45)	S,P,D	1983	C	C	105
Bristol Achievement Tests:																				
Level 1	8:00–9:11	48	25	15	–	21	–	8	35	66	65	30	95	G	55	S,P,Pr	1982	M	M	55
Level 2	9:00–10:11	71	26	15	–	20	–	10	52	70	30	70	100	G	55	S,P,Pr	1982	M	M	56
Level 3	10:00–11:11	64	29	16	–	24	–	–	39	94	20	80	100	G	55	S,P,Pr	1982	M	M	56
Level 4	11:00–12:11	67	30	30	–	18	–	14	29	102	23	77	100	G	55	S,P,Pr	1982	M	M	57
Level 5	12:00–13:11	66	13	22	3	34	4	9	18	115	19	81	100	G	55	S,P,Pr	1982	M	M	57
Profile of Mathematical Skills:																				
Level 1	8:00–13:00	161	28	15	4	6	–	11	136	67	125	63	188	G	(–)	S,P,Pr,D	1979	C	C	143
Level 2	10:00–15:00	188	40	16	4	4	–	8	160	84	137	95	232	G	(–)	S,P,Pr,D	1979	C	C	144
Richmond Tests of Basic Skills:																				
Map Reading and Reading Graphs and Tables	8:00–14:00	23	88	90	–	–	–	–	39	162	0	161	161	G	85	S,P,St,Pr,D	1974	E	E	149
Mathematics Concepts and Mathematics Problem Solving	8:00–14:00	185	11	25	15	7	–	18	62	163	76	156	232	G	65	S,P,St,Pr,D	1974	E	E	150
Moray House: Mathematics Test 7	10:00–12:00R	52	12	5	–	23	1	–	19	74	36	29	65	G	45	S	1970	n.a.	M	131
Chelsea Diagnostic Mathematics Tests:																				
Algebra	12:00–15:11	–	–	10	28	–	–	–	22	16	17	13	30	G	(40)	D,L	1984	*	M	63
Fractions 1	11:00–13:11	28	–	2	–	–	–	–	16	14	8	20	28	G	(30)	D,L	1984	*	M	64
Fractions 2	13:00–15:11	26	–	3	1	–	–	–	12	18	9	17	26	G	(30)	D,L	1984	*	M	65
Graphs	12:00–15:11	24	–	–	–	4	–	–	7	21	–	24	24	G	(45)	D,L	1984	*	E	66
Measurement	11:00–14:11	–	8	25	–	–	–	–	2	31	–	25	25	G	(60)	D,L	1984	*	E	67

Name	Age Range	Content — Domain						Content — Process			Content — Context		Total Items	Administration	Time (untimed)	Form of Scores	Latest Revision	Cost — Specimen	Cost — Each Test	Page
		Number	Measurement	Space	Algebra	Logic	Statistics	Recall	Technique	Comprehension	Abstract	Concrete								
Number Operations	9:00–15:11	14	–	–	–	–	–	4	–	14	–	14	14	G	(40)	D,L	1984	*	M	68
Place Value and Decimals	11:00–15:11	38	4	3	–	–	–	–	34	7	30	9	39	G	(60)	D,L	1984	*	E	69
Ratio and Proportion	12:00–15:11	20	2	–	–	–	–	–	–	22	–	20	20	G	(40)	D,L	1984	*	M	70
Reflection and Rotation	12:00–15:11	–	8	41	–	–	–	–	1	48	–	41	41	G	(60)	D,L	1984	*	E	71
Vectors	13:00–15:11	18	31	39	7	–	–	–	5	90	9	44	53	G	(60)	D,L	1984	*	E	72
Nottingham Number Test (See also Leicester Number Test)	9:01–11:00	79	2	6	–	10	–	18	59	20	78	10	88	G	(55)	S,P,D	1973	C	M	134
Number Test DE	10:06–12:06	40	–	6	14	14	–	–	15	59	44	6	50	G	(50)	S	1970	C	M	139
APU Arithmetic Test	11:00–18:11	48	2	6	–	7	11	3	29	42	39	21	60	G	25	P	1976	C	C	19
SRA Arithmetic Index	14:00–19:00	54	–	–	–	–	–	–	47	7	53	1	54	G	(25)	P,C	1968	O	O	158
Senior Mathematics Test	16:00–18:00	22	–	15	13	10	1	1	31	29	25	25	50	G	45	S	1963	C	M	155

Footnote

* A specimen for the whole series cost £16.95 in 1985, and would therefore be rated E. Averaged across each test, it would be C.